DATE DUE

FEB 28 1994	
JUL - 6 1995	

BRODART, CO.   Cat. No. 23-221-003

Stage Make-Up Techniques

Stage Make-up Techniques

by
Martin Jans

and additional material by
William-Alan Landes

PLAYERS PRESS, Inc.
P.O. Box 1132
Studio City, CA 91614-0132

PLAYERS PRESS, Inc.
P. O. Box 1132
Studio City, CA 91614-0132, U.S.A.

ACKNOWLEDGEMENTS

Publisher and Authors appreciate the assistance of the
following:
Robert Bluver, Mehron, Inc. photos for pages 61 and 81.
Dana Nye, Ben Nye Makeup, photos for page 82.
Paula Hoffman, Shaun Russum and Don Agey for
modeling.
Sharon Gorrell for typeset and layout of new and revised
pages.
Special thanks to Players U.S.A. and its members for
supplying make-up kit supplies, prosthetics, costumes
and photos for INDIAN TALES and THE WIZARD OF OZ.
Players U.S.A. Costume designs by Marjorie E. Clapper;
Make-up designs by William-Alan Landes.

Simultaneously Published
U.S.A., U.K., Canada and Australia

Printed in Hong Kong

Library of Congress Cataloging-in-Publication Data

Jans, Martin.
    Stage make-up techniques / by Martin Jans ;
additional material by William-Alan Landes.
       p. cm.
  ISBN 0-88734-621-9
    1. Theatrical makeup.   I. Landes, William-Alan.   II. Title.
PN2068.J36   1993
792'.027--dc20
                                              92-56429
                                               CIP

Contents

Introduction

Stage make-up uses many different techniques, from painting and colouring the face to create additional lines and folds, to changing the texture of the skin with powders and dyes. This is usually done to depict a particular character or role in a play. A wide variety of materials is used to create these different heads.

Even in classical times in Egypt and Greece, for example, as well as in even older civilisations, such as ancient China and the Papuas, faces were made up to change the shape or for decoration. Modern make-up is based on the visual effect of light and dark, as in the technique used by Rembrandt, Frans Hals and Jan Steen.

An important aspect of natural make-up is the study of faces in the street, on the bus or the train.

The details to look at include the lines on the face, the hollows and curves of the face, and any distinctive features such as a noticeable nose, mouth, eyebrows or eyes.

This book deals with the basic techniques, covering anatomy, light and colour, shadows and highlighting, as well as the plastic techniques; a number of faces are described in detail with numerous clear illustrations.

The book does not aim to be comprehensive, but it does provide a concise and general survey of the most common types of make-up. The series of photographs clearly illustrate the step-by-step approach to creating the various characters. The examples described in this book should serve as a basis, and using the techniques explained here – as well as his own imagination – the reader will be able to create personal faces. Personal experience using variations on the ideas presented here is far more valuable than the mere imitation of the photographs. Make-up is an extremely personal craft and when the basic techniques are mastered, the individual imagination is paramount. An inventive and innovatory approach, as well as a critical eye with regard to the results of the make-up, are all absolutely essential for success and a sense of personal satisfaction.

Start with simple faces and slowly build up to more ambitious projects. The art of make-up can only be mastered with a lot of practice, and by developing an objective eye to appraise the results.

The book also devotes some attention to questions such as how to make glatzan caps, rubber wounds, false noses, beards and hairpieces. The materials required are usually readily available, as are the many ready-to-wear articles, from chemists or joke shops.

The visual method used in the book makes it particularly suitable for schools, courses, amateur dramatics and carnival organisers, as well as for individual use.

Beginners will find it easy to use for their first endeavours, but more advanced students of make-up will also find many useful tips.

Tools and materials

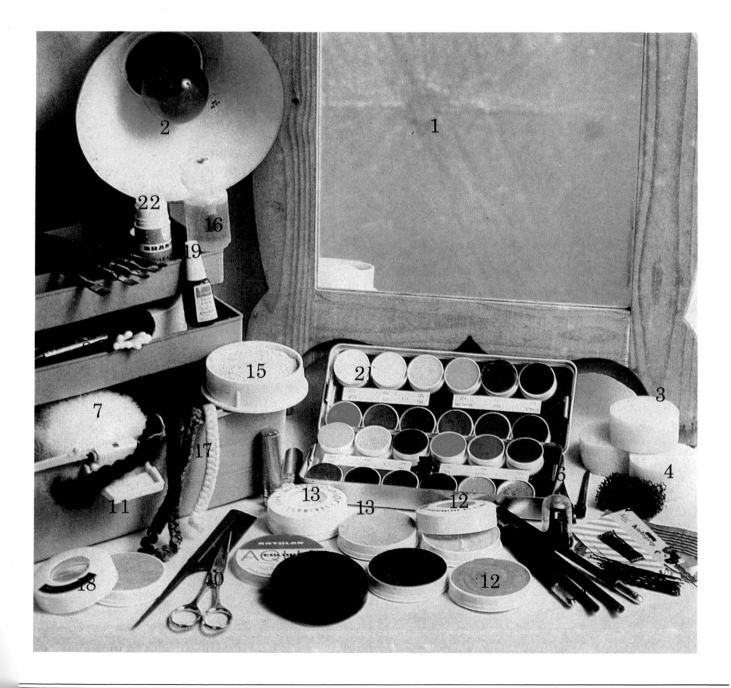

Tools

Mirror and light (see photograph 1 and 2)

A mirror and good lighting are very important for successful make-up. The person being made up should sit straight in front of the mirror so that his face is in the light. The mirror may be fastened onto the wall or placed on the dressing table. The latter is preferable as it is more mobile. An ordinary mirror with one or two folding stands can be used. The best size is 60 x 40 cm.

The mirror should be placed so that the person who is doing the make-up, standing next to the subject, always has a good and complete view of the latter's face.

The results should be constantly checked in the mirror.

The reflection in the mirror gives a good indication of the effect produced at a distance; what can be seen in the mirror is at twice the distance – the image goes from the face to the mirror and from the mirror back to the eyes of the make-up artist. To get an even better impression of the effect of distance on the make-up, screw up your eyes and look through the eyelashes. This gives more or less the impression that is produced on a stage.

For the lighting it is possible to use an angle-poise light attached to the back or side of the mirror.

A 60 watt bulb is sufficient for theatre or street theatre make-up.

The rest of the equipment required includes:

Sponges (see photograph: 3)

A number of small sponges are needed for applying a basic colour. These sponges should be made of plastic foam with small pores, and they should have a slightly greasy feel. They should be round, about 3 cm thick and have a diameter of 6 cm.

Stippling sponge (see photograph: 4)

This is a sponge with a coarser structure which is used for the 'five o' clock shadow' effect and/or to suggest the structure of fine veins. The sponge can be cut into a rounded shape so that there are no hard lines or stripes in the make-up.

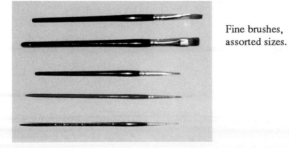

Fine brushes, assorted sizes.

Fine brushes (see photograph: 5)

A number of fine brushes in various widths are needed.

These should be made of flat sable hair. Special make-up brushes are also available, but flat sable hair artists' brushes are quite adequate, although the handles are usually too long. To use them properly they can be shortened to 18 cm (cut off and sharpened to a point with a pencil sharpener).

The most usual widths are:
no. 8 or 0,4 cm for lip seal;
no. 10 or 0,7 cm for shadows of folds or eye shadows;
no. 14 or 0,9 cm for plain shadows or highlights.

Powder puffs (7)

The best powder puffs are made from swan's down. They are difficult to obtain, though they should be available from a good cosmetic shop.

Powder brush

This is a broad soft brush used to remove excess powder from the face.

Three Powder Brushes.

Pointed comb (9)

Not a steel point, but a point made of the same material as the comb.

Scissors (10)

A good pair of hairdressing scissors about 15 cm long.

Chamois

A piece of chamois leather about 10 x 15 cm.

Make-up case (11)

A fishing basket is ideal to use as a make-up case, and all the materials and tools can be kept in it. These baskets usually have two or three hinged trays divided into compartments.

Materials

Make-up

There are two sorts of make-up, i.e., greasepaint or cream-based make-up, and water based make-up or pancake. The difference between the two is: **Greasepaint** (12) is a cream that comes in a box or tube. It does not cover so well but is easier to blend in, and powder should be used to fix it. It is easier to use shadows, highlights or contrasting colours on this base, and these can be blended in better.

Pancake (13) is less easy to use but covers better than greasepaint. It is more difficult to use other colours on top and blend them in, but as it has a matt effect it does not need powdering.

Both types of make-up are resistant to perspiration.

It is advisable to buy a few samples of each type in natural basic colours. Basic colours mean skin colours: lighter, darker, redder or more yellow, depending on the final effect required. It is not really possible to say exactly which basic colour should be used for men, women, older people and children, as this depends entirely on the character that is being created, the subject's own skin colour, the colour of the environment, lighting and distance. There are no fixed standard colours. However, in general one might say that:

- a pinky brown or neutral make-up colour is used for women and children;
- medium brown and slightly darker and brown shades for men;
- ivory and pale shades for older people;
- yellowy brown for Asiatics;
- reddish brown for Arabs and Indians;
- dusty brown or greenish brown for vagrants and gypsies.

When pancake is used, the bold colours such as yellow, green, blue, purple etc. are used for fantasy faces.

Some greasepaint shadow and highlight should be bought; these are available on palettes containing twelve or twenty-four colours.

Pencils (14)

Dermatographic pencils are very soft greasy pencils. The lines can easily be smudged. They are available in a number of different colours, such as light and dark brown, black, white, old and young red, and blue and green.

Powder (15)

The best is a neutral light transparent powder.

Mastic (16)

This is adhesive for beards, used for sticking beards, wigs and moustaches to the face. It usually comes in a bottle with a small brush on the bottle top.

Crêpe hair (17)

Woollen crêpe is wool which has been braided into a hank; it can be pulled and combed and then stuck to the face in the form of beards, eyebrows, moustaches etc. It is available in many different colours such as light brown, dark brown, blond, blackish grey, brownish grey, black, brown and red.

Nose putty (18)

This is a type of modelling clay that is skin coloured and is used for altering the shape of the nose, and/or making warts, wounds, chins, casts on eyes etc.

Tooth varnish (19)

This is the liquid which comes in a small bottle and is used on the teeth. It can be black to create the impression of missing teeth, and is also available in white, brown and gold.

Artificial blood

This is a red liquid substance that is used for blood.

Make-up remover

A sort of vaseline used to remove greasepaint. Pancake is more easily removed with soap and water.

Acetone

This is used to remove the remains of mastic and for the edges of a bald head.

Soap

A piece of soap for washing the hands, and a sponge, also used to remove false eyebrows and hair from the temples.

Hairgrips

Both slides and pins are needed. There should be some large sized pins and small ones for the fringe.

Stocking cap

A small cap can be made from the top edge of a nylon stocking.

Latex solution

Liquid rubber used to make skull cap moulds and false noses.

Glatzan

Liquid polymer used to make very thin skull caps.

Specialty Materials: Ventilated Hair, beards or moustaches; prosthetic facial appliances.

Theoretical aspects

Anatomy

To produce a good make-up it is necessary to be very familiar with the anatomy of the skull and the position of all the facial and neck muscles. The facial muscles are of primary importance in determining a person's appearance. As people get older these muscles sag and the skin falls away from the face and becomes thinner.

1. *Bones of the forehead* The bones of the forehead with two protrusions (1a), the width of the forehead (1b), and the eyebrow arches (1c). 1a and 1c are the most pronounced parts of the forehead.
2. *Temples* These are on either side of the forehead, forming a slight hollow together with the other bones.
3. *Bones of the nose* There is only the bone which forms part of the skull above the nose, as the rest of the nose consists of cartilage.
4. *Eye sockets* The eyes lie in these hollows or holes in the skull.
5. *Cheekbones* These are the protruding bones under the eye sockets.
6. *Nostrils* The more or less flexible cartilage of the nose runs over these hollows, and this cartilage determines the shape of the nose.
7. *Upper jaw* The teeth are set in this rigid bone.
8. *Lower jaw* A hinged bone which also contains teeth. It can be subdivided into the chin bone (8a), the corners of the jaw (8b) and the hinge (8c).

As a result the skull determines appearance to a greater extent. It is therefore particularly important to be aware of the hollows in the skull when making someone up to look older. In older people the skin follows the contours of places where there are hollows or receding areas in the skull, while it does not do so in protruding areas.

Skull
The skull consists of a number of bones which cannot move individually and are fused together, and one moving part, viz., the lower jaw. The facial bones of the fused parts contain the following important bones:

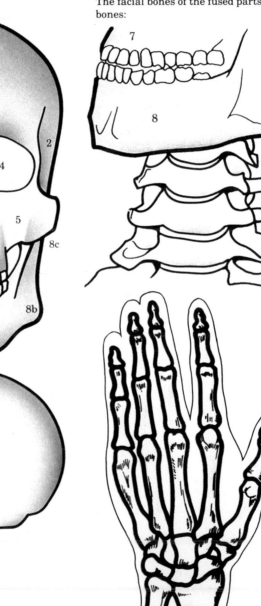

Neck structure
The bone structure of the neck is also important when making up the neck. The cartilaginous larynx lies in front of the vertebrae.

Bone structure of the hand
Note the difference in thickness of the joints in the fingers and the muscles and tendons.

Muscles

The muscles of the head can be subdivided into facial muscles and mimic muscles. It is not necessary to name all the muscles here and we will discuss only those that are important from the point of view of make-up because of the sagging effect of age.

1. *The forehead muscle* This muscle causes the forehead to frown, and pulls up the eyebrows. In older people the forehead is wrinkled.
2. *The eyebrow muscles* These pull the eyebrows inwards and downwards, creating horizontal lines at the base of the nose.
3. *Thin nose muscle* This pulls the skin above the base of the nose down, thus causing horizontal lines at the base of the nose.
4. *Eye sphincter muscle* This muscle has a number of different effects: the upper part shuts the eyelid, the lower part pulls the skin of the cheek upwards, especially at the outer corner of the eye, causing the so-called 'crow's feet'.
5. *Muscles of the upper lip and the side of the nose* The upper lip and the sides of the nose are pulled up by this muscle.
6. *Cheek bone muscle* This muscle serves to raise the lower jaw.
7. *Upper lip muscle* This muscle pulls up the outer part of the upper lip and the corners of the mouth.
8. *Trumpet muscle* This presses the cheeks against the molars and pulls the corners of the mouth away and outwards.
9. *Cheek chewing muscle* This muscle serves to raise the lower jaw.

10. *Chin muscle* This presses the skin of the chin up, producing a point. Lines in the chin are made by this muscle.
11. *Mouth sphincter muscle* This muscle allows the lips to form an 'O', and also shuts the mouth. When this muscle sags, a fold in the corners of the mouth results.
12. *Laughing muscle* This pulls the corners of the mouth outwards and forms the mouth into a long thin line.
13. *The muscle which pulls the corners of the mouth down*
14. *The muscle to raise the ear* This pulls the ear up.
15. *Muscle in the back of the head* This smoothes away the wrinkles in the muscles in the forehead.

Neck muscles

16. *Pectoral, collar bone and mammary muscle* These turn and bend the head.
17. *The wide neck muscle* This muscle pulls up the skin of the neck and also pulls down the lower jaw.
18. *Monk's head muscle* This provides a join to the back of the head but does not have a direct effect on the head itself.
19. *Temple chewing muscle* This muscle raises the lower jaw and also pulls it backwards.

Hand muscles

The muscles and veins of the hand. The hands are important in portraying a character, especially older and bony types.

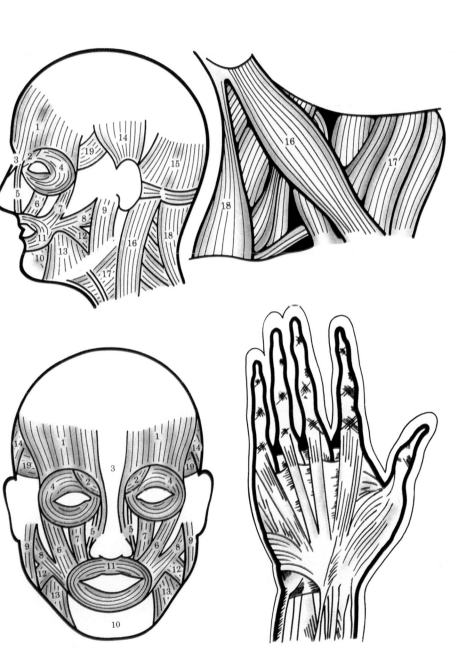

Colour

Colour is a force of radiation. In principle, colour does not exist – molecular surfaces exist. When light falls on these, the molecules absorb the various different rays of colour to which they are receptive.

If particular molecules are missing, e.g., those receptive to green, the green wavelengths are reflected and we perceive the surface as being green. If this area is illuminated with a red light, it looks black because there is no green in red light and therefore no green can be reflected. If no colour wavelength is absorbed at all, the surface appears to be white, as all the rays are reflected. If all the rays are absorbed, then the surface looks black.

The rays of light themselves have no colour but they are 'translated' into colour in the brain via the retina. Distinct colours are known as material colours, and these include the so-called primary colours. These cannot be composed by mixing different colours, and cannot be divided into other colours.

The primary colours are:
– red
– yellow
– blue.

A mixture of these three colours produces a dark brownish grey. Mixing two primary colours produces a secondary colour, which is the complementary colour of the third colour. Thus a mixture of a primary colour and a secondary colour also produces the above-mentioned dark grey.

The complementary colour of red is green (blue + yellow); the complementary colour of yellow is purple (red + blue); and the complementary of blue is orange (red + yellow).

The complementary colours are evoked by the brain when a colour is seen. For example, if you look at a green colour field and quickly shut your eyes, the same field is seen in red, and vice-versa.

For a proper understanding of the different colours a colour circle is shown below. This is built up as follows:
a. the primary colours – cannot be separated;
b. the secondary colours – composed of two primary colours;
c. the tertiary colours – composed one primary and one related secondary colour.

In the colour circle the yellow/purple axis provides the greatest contrast, and this consists of one primary and one secondary colour. The axis perpendicular to this orange/red-blue/green is a cold/warm contrast.

Tertiary colours and other mixtures can be influenced towards cold or warmth by the neighbouring colours.

A good understanding of colours helps you to use colours properly and in a balanced way in make-up, so that the colours complement each other and do not detract from each other. The colour of the lighting in which the make-up is seen also has a great influence on the effect of the colours used.

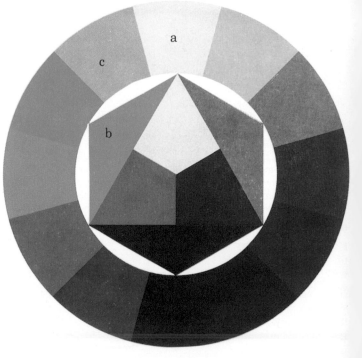

Lighting

What kind of light?

Light is formed by rays of light of many different colours with different wavelengths, though one particular colour is always dominant, both in daylight and with the different types of bulb that may be used.

It is important to know in what sort of lighting the make-up will be seen. If it is at all possible, the make-up should be applied in lighting similar to that when it will be seen. With regard to this, the following questions arise: First: what sort of lighting is there and what is its colour? Secondly: how much light is there? Thirdly: where does the light come from?

Various different types of lighting are commonly used and each produces its own colour and atmosphere.

For example, a light bulb produces a much more yellowy light than a fluorescent or neon light. This should be taken into consideration in choosing the make-up to be used. The question is, what effect the dominant colour has on the colour of the make-up (see the colour circle); the effect can be reinforced or diminished. The lighting may be so strong that the intended effect of a particular colour in the make-up may be lost.

The following lighting conditions and most common types of bulb are:

1. *Daylight*. The clearest but also the most revealing light. If the make-up is to be used in daylight, it should also be applied in daylight. In these conditions the colour blue is dominant.

2. *Electric light bulb*. These bulbs have a warm yellow glow. Shades of purple may look rather grey, and reddish hues will lose some of their intensity. Blue colours acquire a greenish tinge. This applies to an even stronger extent in candlelight.

3. *Fluorescent light*. This light produces a blue background colour, i.e., a cold atmosphere. All colours seem less intense, and orange can seem grey. Blues are intensified.

4. *Spotlight*. This usually has a blue/white colouration. Reddish colours are intensified and the make-up must be well defined as everything can seem rather pale.

5. *Halogen* (studio lighting). Halogen light is a merciless white light that has a bleaching effect on all colours and makes the face seem very flat. It is essential to emphasize the make-up to counteract this effect.

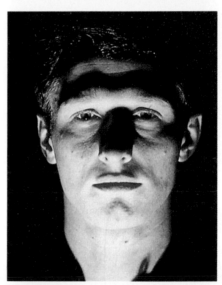

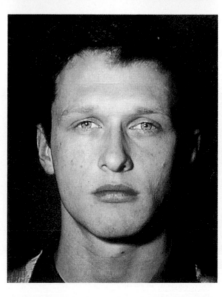

Lighting:

1. *Lighting from above*. If the lighting only comes from above, you must take into account the shadows formed by raised or pronounced parts of the face. For example, the eyes may disappear in the shadows of the arches of the eyebrows. There are also dark shadows on the cheeks under the cheekbones, a shadow of the nose on the upper lip and a shadow of the upper lip in the corners of the mouth. In this case it is better to highlight these areas than shade in the areas mentioned above.

2. *Footlights*. When this kind of lighting is used on its own, it has a very strong effect on the face, almost deforming it by highlighting parts which normally never receive any light, e.g., the underside of the chin, the underside of the nose, and the underside of the arches round the eyes. This should be taken into account, but no special make-up should be used as this would give an extremely unnatural effect.

3. *Stage lighting*. These are usually spotlights in the theatre. They give the best lighting for the face. When they are placed at varying heights and distances there should be no problems with shadows.

1
Clown in normal lighting. Note the primary colours used in this make-up: red, blue and yellow with green as a blending colour.

Coloured light

If coloured lights are to be used, the colour and intensity should be checked by placing a sheet of white paper in front of the light. The information produced should be taken into account when determining the basic colour of the make-up, the additional make-up and highlights.

If different lighting conditions are to be used, the most common of these should be used as a base and the make-up should be as neutral as possible.

2
When red light is used for lighting, colours like blue and green become very dark or black because they are not related to red. White and yellow appear to be the same colour because they reflect the same amount of red.

3
Blue light turns blue black, and yellow green. Reddish colours become almost black and only blue seems lighter.

4
Lighting with a yellow light is most similar to white light and produces reasonably accurate colours. Only blue and green become slightly darker.

5
Under green light only green appears as green. Red looks dark brown. Obviously white parts reflect the green. In green light a naked face looks ill.

The amount of light

The amount of light determines the degree of contrast to be used on shadows and highlights. When there is little light, a slight contrast can seem very heavy, but when there is a lot of light the make-up can be applied using more contrast, as the contrast tends to disappear in the strong light and the face can seem faded.

Indirect lighting

Both footlights and spotlights can light up the face via a reflecting white area. This lighting is usually softer and more subtle than direct lighting. It is often used in photography and/or films. When this lighting is used the make-up should be as soft and detailed as possible and all the colours should be as natural as possible.

All these lighting and colour factors should be taken into account when applying the make-up to obtain the best results. It is also important to consider the colour of the clothes to be worn, particularly when they are dyed or a wig is being worn. The make-up can look completely different if the colour radiates too much light, or as a result of optical absorption.

Warmth and coldness

The use of colour in make-up to add to the depiction of a character can be roughly divided into warm and cold colours. The warm colours are those which are based on red with no mixture of blue, or in which red and/or yellow predominate (see the beginning of this chapter).

It is therefore important to have a good idea of the interpretation of a character. A sly, calculating figure will project his character more forcefully with a choice of a cold colour, while a sympathetic character needs warm colours. To achieve this effect any colour can create a different tone with a colder or warmer shade. In doing this the basic colour continues to exist. The tone of the colour becomes warmer by stippling some red onto the basic colour or the foundation, and blending it thoroughly into the foundation.

In this way a sickly impression can be created by mixing in a little green with the pale base. These changes in tone are most successfully achieved using greasepaint. It is much more difficult to achieve the same effects with pancake and a great deal of practice is required.

The colour which has been added should not be predominant and again it is important to apply it carefully with the use of a great deal of contrast. If a particular colour effect was used in the foundation, the shadowing and highlighting should be adapted to this effect. Colours always work differently when combined with other colours or in different lights, and this should never be forgotten. They can enhance or detract from each other. In addition, colour can work in two ways: in the right place it can appear as the desired colour, but in the wrong place it can appear as an undesirable shadow or patch of light.

Orientation

You should get the best possible view of the head to be made up. The important factors to remember are:
1. the character;
2. the expression;
3. the light in which the character will appear;
4. the colour of the costume;
5. the colour of the environment or decor;
6. the aim of the make-up.

Using this information, make a picture or sketch of the make-up and work, using this as an example.

Light and dark

In addition to the effects of colour and light there are also the effects of adjacent light and dark planes.

Paintings by the old masters which were mentioned above are also based on this principle. Light parts are more prominent, and if particular parts of the face are to be emphasized, these should be made lighter. This is known as highlighting. If other parts of the face are meant to be receding or less prominent, these should be darker than the areas immediately around them. This is known as shadowing. The stronger the contrast between light and dark, the stronger the optical effect. This does not mean that it is always necessary to work with black and white effects. A small and subtle contrast can sometimes be more effective than the coarse use of heavy colours. Once again it should be remembered that excess leads to unsuccessful results. The proper control of contrast coupled with a good understanding of anatomy produces the best results. The pictures below show the effect of light (highlighting) and dark (shadowing) in a systematic way.

1
A circle with a convex effect created by dark outer edges.
The centre of the circle can be lightened. If the colours merge together evenly, a convex optical effect results, and this can be used, for example, for bumps on the forehead, pimples, swollen cheeks, etc.

2
The effect that is produced in a circle can also be used in a rectangle. The way in which light and dark are used in this rectangle produces the effect of a cylinder. This effect can be used for the make-up of noses and the arches of eyebrows.

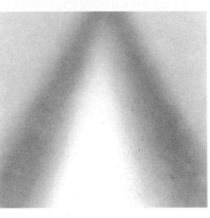

3
Using the same effect of shadows, this triangle has the optical effect of a cone. The light in the centre produces a convex effect. By contrast, dark in the centre produces a concave effect.

4
This circle shows how a convex effect can be created by changing round patches of light and dark. The centre is in shadow and merges evenly with the highlighted edge. It is very important that the areas merge evenly. This effect can be used to create sunken cheeks or deep set eyes.

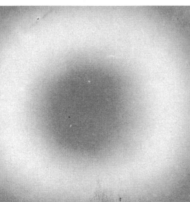

5
A rectangle can also appear to be hollow by shadowing the centre and highlighting the vertical sides. This effect is important when creating shadows on the temples. It is also possible to create sharp or rounded angles by using this technique of light and dark.

6
This illustration shows how a rounded corner can be obtained. The shadow moves from light to dark and back again. On the face this is important for gentle folds in the skin.

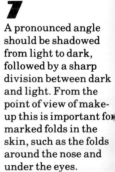

7
A pronounced angle should be shadowed from light to dark, followed by a sharp division between dark and light. From the point of view of make-up this is important for marked folds in the skin, such as the folds around the nose and under the eyes.

Basic techniques

General
The use of a protective cream under the make-up is no longer necessary because modern make-up is of such good quality that it does not harm the skin.

Foundation
Both greasepaint and pancake are applied with a sponge. This sponge should be slightly damp. A little make-up is taken from the container and applied to the face with brushing movements from the middle of the face towards the sides and from the top downwards in long horizontal strokes, beginning with the forehead and going down over the eyes, nose, cheeks, mouth and chin. The make-up should on no account be applied too thickly. The subject's own skin colour also determines the colour of the make-up and the natural effect. The pores should remain visible. It is important to apply make-up in a thin, regular layer, as a thick application of make-up creates a patchy effect in bright light. For this reason the make-up should be properly blended into the hairline so that there is no obvious borderline (creating a mask effect).

This also applies to the neck area. Do not stop at the edge of the jaw but merge the make-up into the neck. If you wish to change the tone slightly, the desired colour can be created by stippling onto the foundation and merging it in. The tone should then be adapted to the shadows and highlights.

Moreover, it is not advisable to use protective creams as this makes it difficult to apply the make-up properly. It can easily become stripy and there is a risk of smudging.

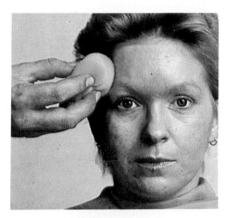

Shadows
After the foundation has been applied the shadows can be put in, followed by the highlights. The following colours can be used as shadows, depending on the character to be portrayed:

brown (in various shades)
green - moss green
grey
blue
violet
soft red - carmine

1

Using a brush, apply some dark make-up to the places where shadows or folds have to be added.

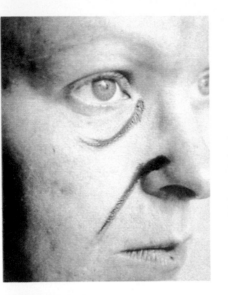

2

Using a finger, this dark make-up is merged thoroughly with the foundation in all directions so that the shadow and the foundation merge together gradually. To create a sharp shadow contrast, as in the nose and the fold in the nose, the shadow only has to be thoroughly merged down one side.

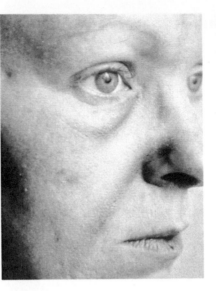

3

Highlighting
The highlights are then applied with a brush adjacent to the shadows. The highlights should be applied in the same colour as the foundation and the shadowing, e.g., pinky white, greenish white or greyish white.

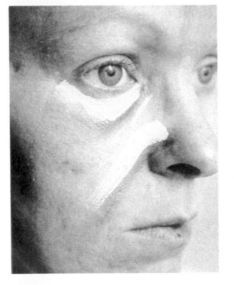

4

Using a finger, this light-coloured make-up is also blended into the foundation and with the shadowing. The shadowing and the highlights should not be blended too much into each other, and care should be taken that the intensity and the colour are not lost.

5

Florid effect
Using a coarse-grained sponge, a little carmine make-up is applied in places where the florid effect might appear naturally. After taking the make-up from the container, rub the sponge over a palette or glass plate, dividing the make-up carefully.

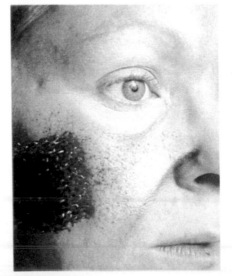

6

Five o'clock shadow effect
A sponge can be used in the same way to create the effect of an unshaven face, using very dark brown pancake. Do not use too much water on the sponge or the make-up. Try to observe the beard growth of people around you. You will also observe that some men grow hair under the chin.

Powdering

When using greasepaint, you should finish off with powder. The powder serves to stabilise the make-up and prevents the face from shining. A good light neutral powder is patted onto the make-up with a swans' down powder puff – it should never be rubbed – and the excess powder is then brushed away with a powder brush. Never skimp on the powder, for it keeps the make-up in place and prevents fading. When the powder has been applied and the excess brushed away, it can be more firmly fixed to the foundation with a clean damp sponge. This fixes the foundation but it does slightly diminish the powdered effect.

Powder should have a very fine consistency. The finer it is, the more transparent the effect becomes.

Coarse powder covers up and the effect of the make-up is largely lost. The powder should always be of a lighter colour than the foundation as the final colour will be too dark otherwise.

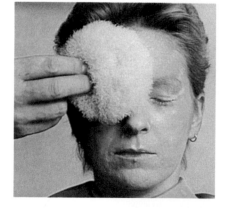

Eyebrows

Eyebrows are extremely important in a facial expression and for characterisation. An incorrectly drawn eyebrow can ruin the entire make-up, or mean that the desired character fails to be properly expressed. The eyebrows should not merely be drawn on as an arched line as this produces a hard and unnatural impression. It is better to fill in the eyebrow as an arch, using a pointed dermatographic pencil. Now draw diagonal, slightly curved lines slanted towards the end of the eyebrow so that superficially they look just like hairs.

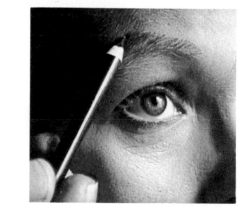

If the eyebrows can retain their natural shape and only need to be drawn in, the little lines must be drawn in following the natural line of the hairs. If they have to change shape, the upper or lower edge should be a sharp line to indicate the new shape. If necessary, draw in the lines upwards as well as downwards as follows: draw in downwards starting just above the edge of the natural eyebrow. Draw in upwards using the pencil from the lower edge of the subject's eyebrow.

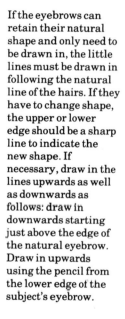

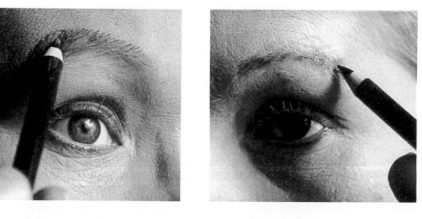

1
First against the grain.

Soaping the eyebrows
If the eyebrows are to be higher or narrower than the natural eyebrows, they should be rubbed with the corner of of a wet piece of soap.

2
Then with the grain flat against the skin.

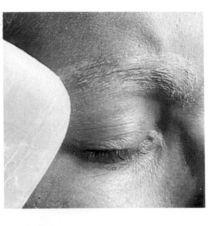

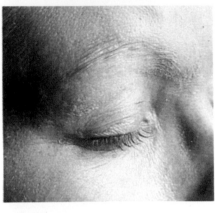

3
Leave the soap to dry.

4
Pat in some foundation.

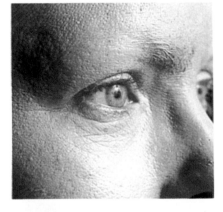

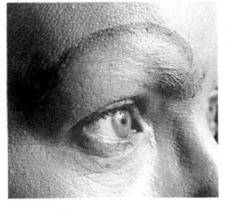

5
The eyebrow is then drawn in an arch at the required height.

6
Eyeliner
Using a dark dermatographic pencil, the eye is outlined. The pencil should be sharpened to a point. First draw a line as closely as possible along the edge of the eyelash from the inside corner to the outside.

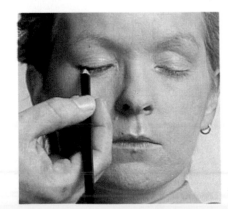

7
Now do the same along the lower eyelashes. The lines should not touch as this reduces the size of the eye.

Making the hands look older
Hands can be an important feature in the make-up and old hands go with an old face. A gypsy or vagrant character should have dirty uncared-for hands.

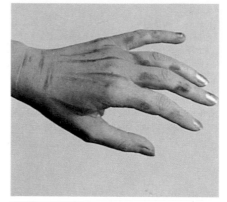

1
After applying the foundation, shadow colours are filled in where there are contours in older people's hands, e.g., on the backs of the hands and on the sides of the fingers.

2
A light colour is then applied and also blended in.

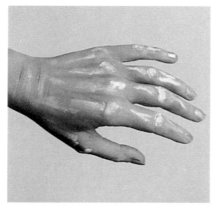

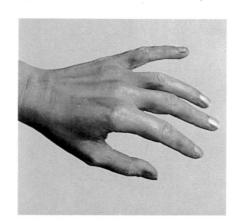

3
A few lines can be drawn on the nails with a pencil to create a wrinkled effect. A pencil line under the nails will create a dirty and/or nicotine-stained effect.

4
Black eye
On a palette or glass plate, mix the colours carmine, yellowish green and blue to create a purple colour.

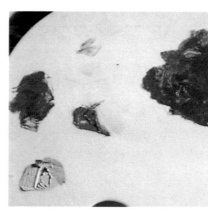

5
This is now patted into the desired area with the fingertips.

6
A few contrasting colours are applied to the area using yellowish green and blue make-up.

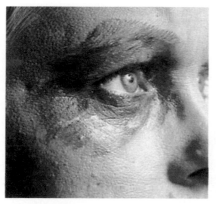

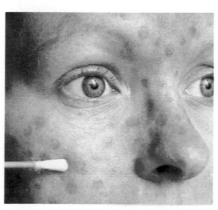

7
Freckles
A freckled effect can be obtained by dabbing some medium brown make-up on the face with a cotton bud. This should be put on in an irregular pattern, not too heavily.

Nose putty

This is a type of skin coloured modelling clay used to change the shape of the face. It should be put onto the face before the make-up is applied, when changes in the facial structure are required.

This will depend on the character. You must take care with the areas in the places which are very mobile in mime, such as the middle of the forehead, the area around the mouth and along the jaw (except for the chin). The edges of the nose putty soon work loose in these places. Nose putty is put on before applying the foundation, but the area where it is to be applied should first be cleaned and any traces of grease removed.

1

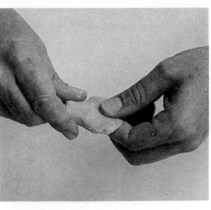

Take a piece of nose putty from the box or stick. Knead it well until it is soft and easy to work.

2

Now use it to create the required shape; in this case, the nose.

3

The nose putty can now be moulded into the final shape round a bent finger. The finger represents the basic shape of the nose itself.

4

The outside of the shape is now smoothed out with a spot of make-up remover. The edges should also be made as thin as possible.

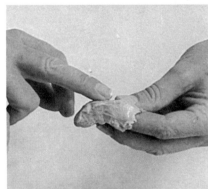

5

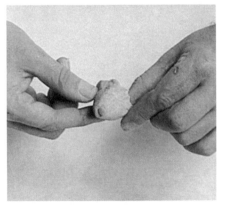

Now the chin is roughly moulded into shape using a well kneaded piece of nose putty. Again the edges should be made as thin as possible and smoothed out with some make-up remover.

6

A little mastic is applied to the area where the nose putty is to be fixed – in this case, the nose – and short strands of crêpe hair are pressed into it.

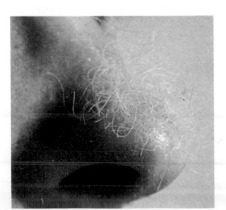

7

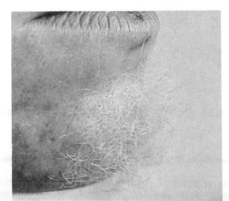

This is also done on the chin. The crêpe hair ensures that the nose putty sticks to the skin better.

8
The nose putty is now firmly pressed onto the crepe hair. Make sure that it is pressed into the right spot as the sticking power is reduced each time it is removed and put back again. Check that the shape and position are correct from the front as well as from the side.

9
Using a drop of make-up remover on the finger, the edges of the nose putty are smoothed out so that they merge evenly with the skin and there are no visible edges or lines. The nose putty is then powdered.

10
The foundation is then applied to the face and the nose putty. Make sure that this foundation is patted in and not rubbed or stroked onto the nose putty.

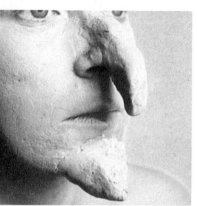
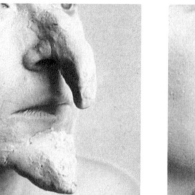

11
Using a fine grained sponge, the pores and/or florid effect can be created, patting carefully. This effect will also help to obscure any remaining visible edges. Make sure that the shape of the putty follows the natural curves of the skin, such as the contours of the nose.

12
Raised eyebrows and cheekbones The nose putty is simply pressed onto the required areas.

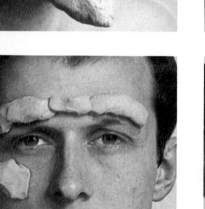

13
The nose putty is then smoothed against the skin and then smoothed out with a drop of grease and covered with make-up.

14
A nose putty cut The nose putty is applied at the required place, not too thickly. 3 mm is sufficient. As far as possible use the natural contours. Again merge into the skin and smooth the putty. Then make up the whole face. (This is not shown here, so that the next step can be more clearly shown.)

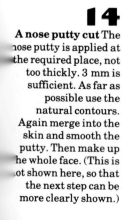
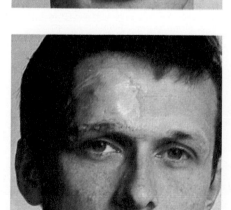
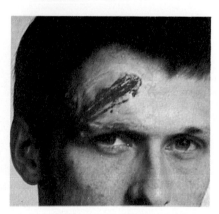

15
With the point of a brush draw a line in the nose putty and fill the line with artificial blood. Also put some along the edges. Leave the blood to run out in streams.

Prosthetics

Rubber (latex) appliances are a convenient alternative to using putty, especially when the make-up must be applied on a repeated basis. They can drastically alter features, create a myriad of characters, and are available for reuse, simplifying the make-up task.

The appliances or pieces, as they are called, should always be attached to clean, dry skin. Spirit gum is the most reliable adhesive. During long performances or where there is a great deal of movement periodic application of adhesive touch-up may be needed. Standard grease paint should not be used on rubber, it will cause it to deteriorate. There are several specially formulated Rubber Mask Grease Paints or Water Soluble make-ups that can be used. If you must use a Cake Make-up always lay a foundation of Rubber grease paint or Castor Oil first, powder and then apply the cake make-up. The mask make-up may still be lighter than your face, so try to blend the color.

The piece can usually be removed by merely pulling it off. The adhesive and make-up should be cleaned from the rubber as soon as possible. It can be pulled or rolled off with the fingers. If Spirit Gum was used then thoroughly clean with alcohol or acetone. The make-up should also be removed with alcohol or acetone.

1. Pinnochio Nose
2. Witch Nose
3. Witch Chin
4/5. Horns
6. Witch Nose
7. Warts
8/9. Large Ears

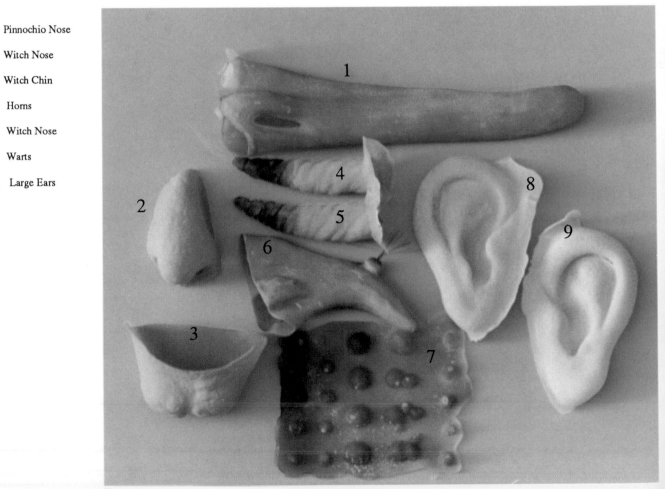

1

Paula thoroughly washes face with an astringent skin cleanser, such as witch hazel.

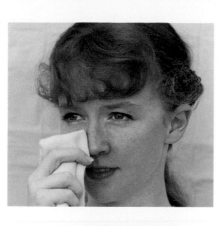

2

Position latex loosely on skin. Trim to suit facial structure.

3

Apply spirit gum to skin, extend spirit gum beyond edges of the piece.

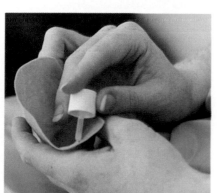

4

Apply spirit gum on interior of the piece. Let it stand to allow spirit gum to become sticky to the touch.

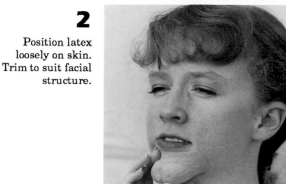

5

Carefully apply piece to desired area. Be sure that edges are pressed flush to the skin.

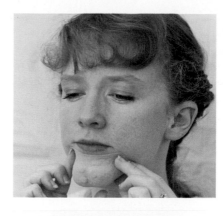

6

Seal edges of piece to the skin.

7

Apply powder on edges to prevent a sticky surface.

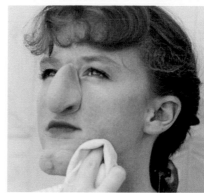

Alternate Nose with hair growing from wart.

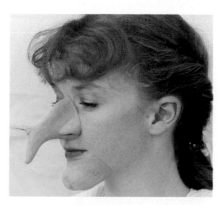

Glatzan

To produce a bald head it is possible to use a latex rubber or plastic skull cap. To make a rubber bald head, a negative impression of the head is needed, together with the required change in shape. This means it is rather complicated to make. The advantage of a latex rubber bald head is that it retains its shape and can be used over long hair that has been put up. However, it is rather difficult to get rid of the edges. A plastic bald head, on the other hand, is extremely thin and can only be used with short hair. The cap fits snugly round the head, taking on the shape of the skull. Any irregularity becomes immediately visible and the cap can easily be damaged by a hairgrip.

Plastic caps are particularly suitable for photographic work. They can be made over a model. The steps for making a plastic skull cap are described below.

1

Materials needed
A non-porous head made of a hard plastic material or glazed pottery or metal (not illustrated), always smaller than the head on which the skull cap will be used. A bowl for the Glatzan, a disposable brush, a tin of polymer, trade name: 'Glatzan'.

2

Apply four layers of liquid plastic to the model from the bowl. Each layer dries in approximately 30 minutes. Always pour just a little in the bowl at a time. Cover the head systematically, as you cannot see where the material has been applied. Thin areas could go into holes when stretched.

3

Keep the opening for the face as small as possible, and the neck as long as possible. The cap stretches on the head and pulls towards the sides. If the opening for the face is too large it will not be possible to cover the sideburns and the hair on the temples.

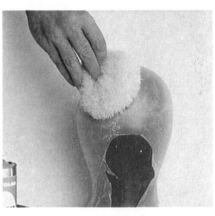

4

When four layers have been applied and have dried, the outside of the cap should be generously and carefully powdered before removing the cap. The powder to be used can be talcum powder or face powder.

5

The plastic cap is loosened from the middle of the back at the bottom, outwards. The inside is powdered bit by bit as soon as it has been loosened.

6

When the edges of the opening for the face have also been loosened and powdered, (the central part in the front remains attached) the cap is pulled away from the model from the back to the front. Make sure that the whole thing is thoroughly powdered

7

The middle of the edge in the front is carefully loosened last of all, while continuing to powder all over.

8

When the cap has been completely removed the inside and outside are again thoroughly patted with the powder puff.

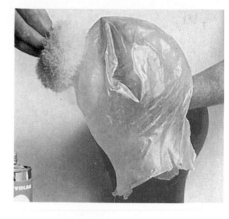

9

The cap can now be put on after the hair has been combed as flat as possible. It is taken by the back edge and pulled over the head from the front.

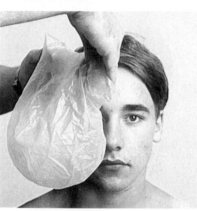

10

Pull the cap as deeply as possible over the head so that no air remains trapped under it. Check that the cap is positioned in the centre of the head with both sides pulled equally forward. The thin edges on the forehead should not be folded double.

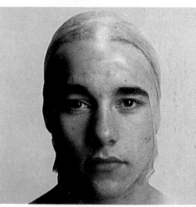

11

The cap can now be cut at the sides to free the ears. Watch the line of the scissors to the front of the ear. It should run up to the join of the ear at the top.

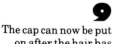

12

The two sides are now laid flat to the front and back of the ear. Make sure that the cut is deep enough and that there are no folds anywhere.

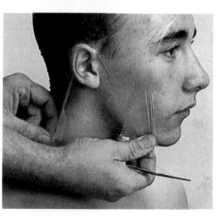

13

Now the side in front of the ear is cut off at a length which generously covers any hair in front of the ear.

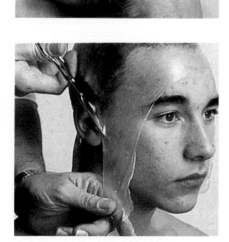

14

This is also done with a part of the edge at the front so that the eyebrows are completely uncovered.

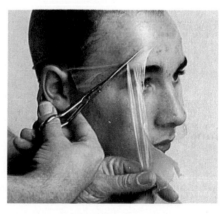

15

The front edge is stuck to the forehead with mastic in the centre. To do this the skin is pressed together between the fingers so that the brush will go under the cap.

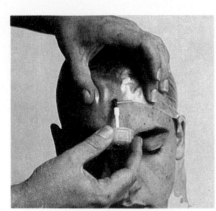

16

Next, stick down the cap at the back of the neck in the centre. To do this the head should be bent right back so that the cap is fully stretched in the normal position.

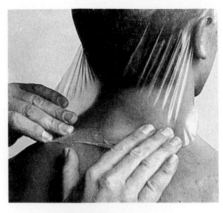

17

With one hand on the nape of the neck and the other hand on the forehead, the head is held right back until the glue has thoroughly set.

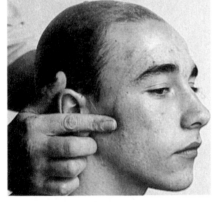

18

Then carefully stick down the sides. The whole edge should be stuck down thoroughly. Any pieces that are not stuck down will be noticeable.

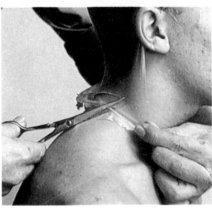

19

Again the cap should be stretched so that there are no folds. It is important to hold down the edges until the glue has thoroughly dried.

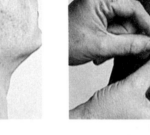

20

The sides at the back now have to be cut off so that the hair is completely covered, but the cap does not have to be stuck down too far to the front. These parts then have to be stuck down tautly.

21

Using a brush dipped in acetone the slightly overlapping edges can be merged with the skin. It is important to be extremely careful as too much acetone can produce holes by dissolving the material.

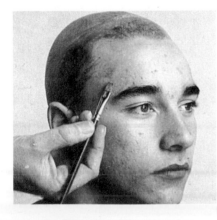

N.B. (The left over pieces of Glatzan can be kept and used for other make-up effects.) The whole head can now be made up in the desired colour. It is best to use pancake. The first layer is applied with brush stroke movements; the second is patted on. The skull cap is taken off by first freeing the back, then over the sideburns, and then by pulling the cap forwards over the head. The cap can be cleaned by washing it on the hand with soap. Dry thoroughly and store it so that it is as open as possible.

Serious injury

Serious injuries can be simply but very effectively simulated with gelatine. Before doing this you must decide what sort of injury it is to be and how serious. Again an over-excessive injury will not look right. The gelatine can be applied directly and modelled on the skin.

1
Requirements
Gelatine powder; (this is industrial gelatine and not leaf gelatine), glycerine, small pan, water, and artificial blood.

2
Equal parts of water and gelatine are mixed together and heated au bain marie. When the gelatine turns into a smooth mixture, the glycerine is added in the proportion of three parts of gelatine to one of glycerine. Finally add a few drops of artificial blood to obtain the correct degree of redness. Mix thoroughly and leave to stand for a while.

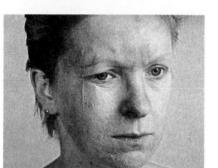
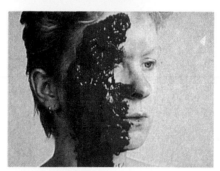

3
Using a lotion, remove all traces of grease from the skin. In the example shown the outer corner of the eye has been covered with a left over piece of glatzan.

4
Reheat the glycerine until it is liquid. Before applying it, first test for heat with a little on the inside of the wrist. Then apply the mixture to the face with a spoon; when it starts to set, build up the structure with the back of the spoon by pressing the spoon in and then pulling it out.

5
Using light-coloured make-up, highlight the thickened areas or those parts which have to stand out.

6
Dark make-up is applied to lower areas or parts which should appear to be deeper.

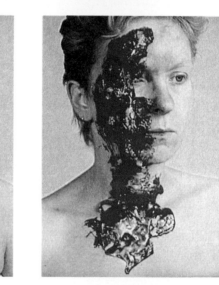
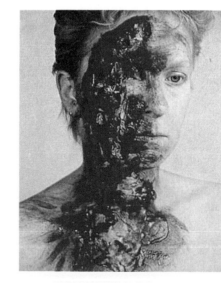

7
Using blood red make-up or artificial blood accentuate some areas and blur the edges.

8
Finally go round the skin surrounding the wound with a fine grained sponge with blood red make-up in order to obtain a slightly glazed effect. The wound and surrounding skin are then thoroughly powdered. It is possible to use the wound a number of times by sticking it onto the face with mastic. After use, melt down in the pan.

Rubber wounds

For small or localised wounds, and even for fast changes, prefabricated rubber wounds can be used. Again it is important to bear in mind what sort of wound is required; for example, whether it is a cut, a slash from a sabre, a gunshot wound, etc. Although these rubber wounds are fairly flexible it is not a good idea to use them on the very mobile parts of the face such as the mouth or eyelids. Things you will need are silipol rubber or latex, a disposable brush, a glass plate, glass bowl and tissues.

1
A little rubber is brushed onto the glass plate with a brush in the basic shape required. It should not be too large. If it has to be cut smaller, this will produce hard edges which cannot be smoothed out.

2
Using the thumb and index finger, roll up pieces of tissue to make up the raised areas. When the first layer is dry and completely transparent, the pieces of tissue are laid on top to form the required shape.

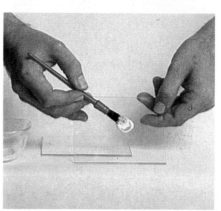

3
This is again covered with a generous layer of rubber. Make sure that when you are applying the next layers the rubber is not drawn too close to the edge of the first layer.

4
All the rolls of tissue should be completely covered by the rubber. Make sure that the rolls do not move about.

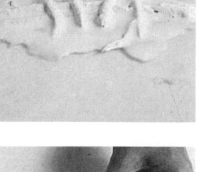

5
When the second layer is completely dry, the third layer is applied, becoming thinner towards the edges. Make sure the rubber is applied against the relief to obtain a diagonal effect.

6
Before taking the wound off the plate, powder thoroughly with talcum or face powder.

7
The rubber is now removed from the glass plate while continually powdering the back.

8
The wound is stuck onto a clean face with mastic. Make sure that the edges are properly stuck down. It is easier to apply the mastic to the back of the wound and round the edges.

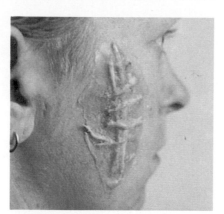

9
Next use a small sponge or brush to smear a little rubber over the edges of the wound. Leave to dry, or if you are in a rush, dry with a hair dryer.

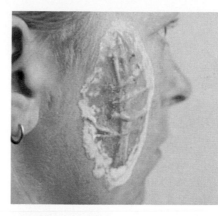

10
When the wound is completely dry, apply the foundation. This should be patted on gently over the wound.

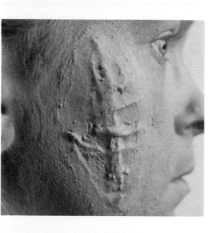

11
Using light coloured make-up accentuate the raised parts of the relief, and on the lower parts use dark or carmine red. If the wound is to look fresh, use a brighter red, and if it is an old wound, use brown instead of red.

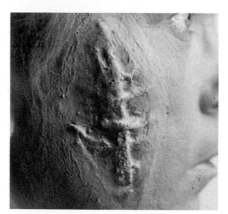

12
This wound is stuck onto the forehead with mastic.

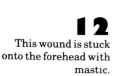

13
The edges are now brushed with rubber to create a smoother transition.

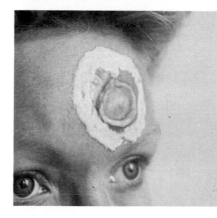

14
The foundation is applied over the skin and the wound.

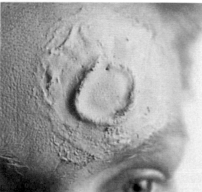

15
Using light, dark and red make-up add some optical relief. Finally, some artificial blood is used to suggest a gunshot wound.

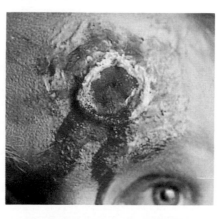

Crêpe hair

1

Crêpe hair consists of long strands of wool or hair that is plaited between two strings and is then boiled and dried. This means that it is very tightly curled. It can be used to make beards, moustaches and eyebrows, which are then stuck onto the face. Take hold of a length of crêpe hair with both hands.

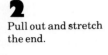

2

Pull out and stretch the end.

3

The string which holds the braided crêpe is cut.

4

The string is pulled out of this length of crêpe.

5

The end of the crêpe hair from which the string has been removed is fanned out.

6

The fanned out end is held between the palm and fingers as wide as possible.

7

The end is slowly removed from the length of crêpe hair.

8

The tuft is now separate from the length of crêpe hair. Keep an eye on the direction of the strands.

9

The tuft is held by the ends.

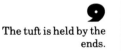

10

The end of the tuft is twisted once halfway round.

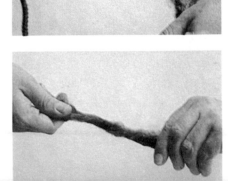

11

Pull the tufts in two lengthways, keeping the strands straight. Pulling the crêpe like this makes it looser and removes the clumps.

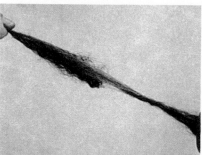

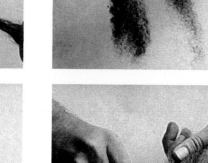

12

The two pulled out tufts are now put together one on top of the other in the same direction, and the process is repeated from the point where it was twisted halfway round until there are no more clumps in the tuft.

13

A tuft of crêpe hair which has been pulled apart three times so that there are no clumps.

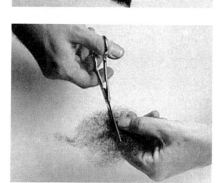

14

The tuft is firmly held in the middle and the ends are combed out.

15

When the tuft is combed out, all the loose hairs are removed. If these were stuck down, the rest would come loose too soon.

16

Twist the tuft into a point at both ends to keep it together, and indicate the direction of the hair. A beard can be stuck on with a collection of these tufts. Keep the tuft between a folded sheet of paper to store it.

17

Before sticking the tuft down, cut through the middle.

18

This gives a straight edge. Crêpe should always be stuck into the mastic with this cut edge.

19

To stick the hairs in a particular direction the tuft should be cut diagonally after being cut through the middle.

20

This tuft of hair has been cut diagonally. When it is stuck on the face it will hang down at an angle, away from the face.

21

The centre front of a goatee or a beard under the lower lip is shaped like a 'W'. From the corner of the mouth down to the centre at an angle, then up to the centre, down again and up to the other corner of the mouth.

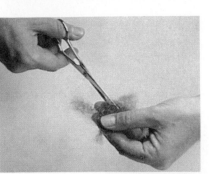

22

This 'W' shape can be cut from the tuft and stuck down as the last part of a beard or goatee.

23

Stubble
Combed crêpe can also be used to make stubble. The crêpe is pressed into a little ball and cut into very short pieces (about 2 mm long).

24

When the crêpe has been cut once the pieces are swept together and cut up again to separate them.

25

Using a brush separate the short pieces of cut-up crêpe so that there are no clumps.

26

Apply mastic, or if possible, stubble paste, to the face in the shape of a beard.

27

With a brush apply some of the short pieces of crêpe hair to the treated areas.

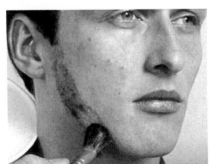

28

Do the whole beard in this way making sure that the crêpe is put on evenly. Remove excess pieces with a sweeping motion of the brush.

29

Eyebrows are always put on over the natural eyebrows. A tuft of crêpe cut through the middle is pressed into the mastic with the cut-off side down.

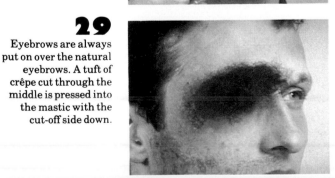

30

When the whole tuft has been pressed down over the natural eyebrow, it is cut into shape. It should not be too long, and the lower edge should be cut along the bottom of the natural eyebrow.

Sideburns, Beard, Moustache

Sideburns or a crêpe beard of any shape are built up in sections.

The beard is stuck down piece by piece from the chin to the sides up to the join of the natural hair in front of the ear. Then the moustache is stuck on.

The sideburns are built up from the sides. The photographs below show how different sorts of sideburns have been created. To show the final shape, the crêpe has been cut to the right shape for each stage. For long sideburns or a beard all the crêpe hair is first cut down and then the whole thing is cut into shape.

2 The tuft is pushed backwards towards the ear and is then cut short into shape. The crêpe should be the same length as the natural hair, especially at the join.

1 To make straight sideburns two tufts of crêpe are stuck down in front of the ear below the natural hair.

4 This is then also cut to the required shape. The shape in this photograph starts off narrow and becomes long and rounded.

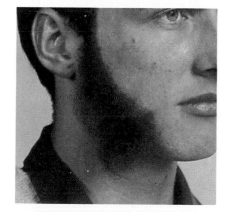

3 For an 1850s sideburn a number of tufts are cut diagonally and stuck down along the line of the jaw, each overlapping the next. Each piece should join on and merge with the sideburn that has already been stuck down.

6 Again the final shape depends on the character required or on taste. The mouth should always be cut free, and the line next to the mouth runs outwards from the cleft under the nose.

5 To make a moustache a few more tufts of hair are added to the sideburns. Note the direction of the crêpe hairs; they should run down diagonally from the mouth.

Ventilated Hair Pieces

In many situations crêpe hair, beards and moustaches are not satisfactory. For close-ups, in movies or television, they are not realistic and for a long run play they are a nuisance. The most convenient and realistic looking beards and moustaches are made of synthetic or real hairs individually knotted onto a net foundation. The process of knotting is known as *ventilation*. The hair actually appears to be growing out of the skin, and the piece can be easily attached and removed. The ventilated piece will last a long time with proper care.

Ventilated hair can be purchased or constructed. For the scope of this book construction is unnecessry. The collection of pieces shown below and used in the accompanying photos were all cut from used/clean hair pieces that had lace fronts and were donated to Players U.S.A. Repertory Theatre Company. Ventilated hair pieces can be purchased from any good make-up or wig supply.

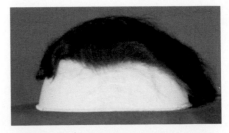

1960's hair style. Ventilated Men's Hair piece.

The favorite of movie stars.

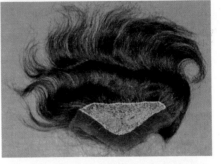

The above hair piece.

The heavy lace is for tape and the fine lace for spirit gum.

Moustaches Ventilated before the lace is trimmmed

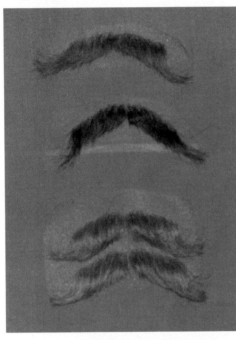

Assorted Moustaches

Beard and Moustache

Trimmed Moustache and Goatee

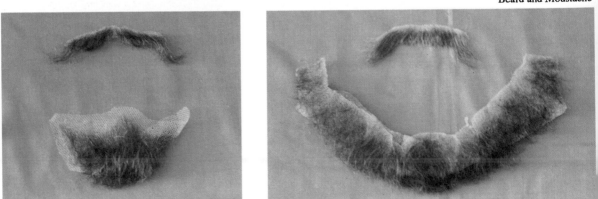

Beards and Moustaches should always be carefully stored so that they will remain clean and the net will not be damaged. Use individual boxes that are large enough so that the hair is not pressed flat.

1

Shaun after cleansing skin with an astringent, such as Witch Hazel.

2

Fit beard to face. Trim lace leaving enough edge to blend into face make-up.

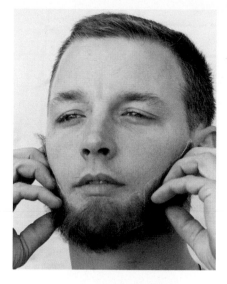

3

Cut and Place double sided toupee tape on beard and moustache.

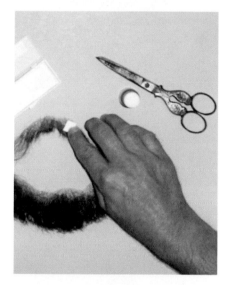

4

Set beard in place.

Brush spirit gum on skin under edges of lace.

5

Set Moustache in place.

Brush spirit gum under edges of lace.

6

Let spirit gum set and become tacky.

Use a clean lint-free cloth to blot lace into spirit gum. Lightly powder edges.

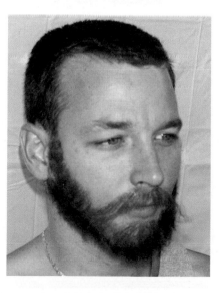

Putting on a wig

1

When the make-up is complete the wig can be put on. First, the hair should be combed down as flat as possible. This can be covered with a small cap made from the top of a nylon stocking. If one end is tied into a knot, this forms a cap with the close fitting edge as an opening.

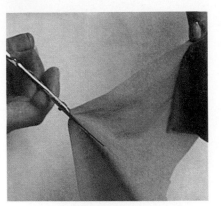

2

The stocking is pulled from the front, back over the hair. It is best to have someone hold it at one point in the front.

3

The stocking is smoothed back at the front right up to the hairline, and fastened with two diagonally crossed hairslides on either side of the forehead and in the nape of the neck. For men the hair is combed back as tightly as possible and also fastened with hairslides.

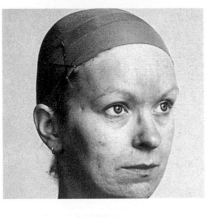

4

The wig is put on from the front to the back over the stocking cap and stuck down to the nape of the neck. Again someone should hold the front edge with one finger.

5

The wig should be pushed back as far as possible, almost to the natural hairline, though none of the subject's own hair should be visible. Hold the front of the wig firmly with one hand while pulling it right down to the neck with the other hand.

6

The wig is kept in place with large hairpins. First slide the pin through the wig to the front.

7

Then flick the pin round and back and slide into the hair under the cap.

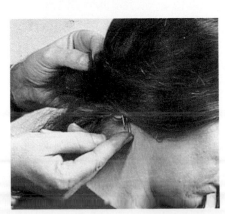

8

The wig will stay in place using four or six pins. Two pins on either side of the forehead, two at the front edge at the temples, and two behind at the neck.

Sisal hairpieces

Sisal is very suitable for fantasy hairpieces and coarser wigs. It can be bought by the pound from any supplier of rope. It is easy to dye using fabric dyes. It does not have to be boiled, as long as it is immersed in boiling water for about 15 minutes. Apart from this, follow the instructions on the packet of dye.

When the sisal has been knotted, it is also easy to curl. Loose curls can be made by rolling lengths of sisal and securing them round hairpins. Tighter curls can be made with curlers to the desired shape. In both cases immerse the sisal in water after curling it, and leave to dry. It is also possible to use a smooth electric hair curler.

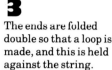
Before starting, hang up a line of string. Then pull a few strands from a thick bunch of sisal.

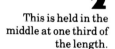
This is held in the middle at one third of the length.

The ends are folded double so that a loop is made, and this is held against the string.

The ends are then pulled through the loop round the string.

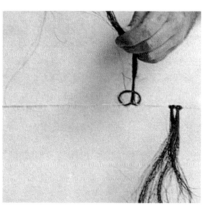
The strand is now fastened to the string by the loop.

The sisal is pulled taut round the string.

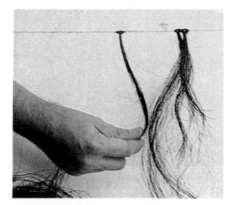

When all the strands have been knotted round the string, it should be thoroughly brushed at the front and back with a coarse hard brush.

Period Hair Styles

A correct hair style can add much to the overall appearance and is probably second only to the actor's period costume. Accuracy becomes more critical as you get closer to the present, whereas a few hundred or even thousand years could easily go unnoticed if you are presenting an Ancient Egyptian style. You may select an older style by ten to twenty years for a special character but never select a style that is even a year ahead of its time. The sketches here are only intended as a rough guide and general outlines for each period. There are countless variations of each style with many styles overlapping from one era to another.

If the character requires a very complicated and specific style it is best to use a wig and relieve yourself of the burden of preparing the hair for each performance. Try to keep your style as simple as possible whenever you use your own hair.

Hebrew

Persian/Mede/Assyrian

Egyptian

Nefertiti Style

Greek

The Ancient Egyptians usually shaved their heads and wore wigs. Although there were many styles the basic outline remained much like the sketches. The simplest solution is to conceal the hair and wear an Egyptian style head-dress. The classic example is the bust of Queen Nefertiti.

The Ancient Greeks tried to simplify their hair styles. Women often piled their hair on the top or back of the head, binding it with ribbons and triangular scarves. The hair was often dressed forward to conceal the forehead. Blonde hair was fashionable and bleaching was common as well as dusting with gold powder. Spiral curls or ringlets were also popular often falling from the top knot at the back of the head. The men combed the hair forward and sometimes curled it.

The Ancient Roman styles were very similar to the Greeks with the women wearing top knots and ringlets and the men combing the hair forward. In the late Roman Empire women became more complicated with extensive use of braids and very tight curls piled extravagantly on top of their heads.

The Medieval period had women covering their hair, after marriage, with a veil or mentoniere (chinstrap). Women also plucked or shaved their hairlines to give themselves higher foreheads. Single women wore their hair long and flowing or tied into long heavy plaits.
Men's hair varied even more than womens; varying by class distinction, from country to country, and even year to year.

The Fifteenth Century hair styles brought a great deal of variety from the middle ages. Women continued to intricately braid and tie their long hair with young unmarried women wearing it freer and longer. The Italian ladies added fashionable cover caps. The men, too, used many of the earlier styles but added the monk cut (i.e. Henry V of England).

The Sixteenth Century saw much of the ladies fashion influenced by Spain. Women brushed their hair high onto their heads, sometimes over pads and wire frames. Curly wigs in the color and style of Elizabeth I were also very popular. Men seemed to free their hair, or brush it off their foreheads, Beards and moustaches became more significant.

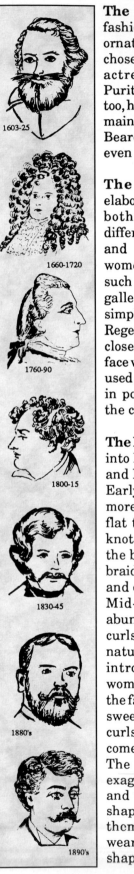

1603-25

1660-1720

1760-90

1800-15

1830-45

1880's

1890's

The Seventeenth Century hair fashions became more varied and ornate for women. The Royalists chose the decorated wired curls like actress Nell Gwynn while the Puritans were severely prim. Men, too, had extremes ranging from curls, mainly wigs, to simply cut and brush. Beards and moustaches took on an even greater importance.

The Eighteenth Century elaborated on the use of wigs for both men and women. Class differences created both frivolous and practical styles. Upperclass women used extensive ornaments such as ribbons, baskets of fruit, galleons, etc., while servants used simple mop caps to cover their hair. Regency women dressed their hair closer to the head and framed their face with curls. Jewelled combs were used extensively. Men's wigs peaked in popularity and began fading by the close of the century.

The Nineteenth Century is broken into Early Victorian, Mid-Victorian and Edwardian.
Early Victorian women favored a more austere style, dressing the hair flat to the head with the early top knot developing into a sort of bun at the back of the head and neat plait braids were often close to the temples and over the ears.
Mid-Victorian women used an abundance of false hair and spiral curls pinned to the back of their natural hair. By the 1890's and the introduction of natural waving, women started to rid themselves of the false pieces and favoured a softer sweep of the hair into various waves, curls, etc. over a top knot that had come forward on the head.
The Edwardian style had heavy exaggerated coiffures needing pads and false hair to achieve the right shape and height. Men had freed themselves of the wig and were wearing their hair shorter, cut, and shaped as the century progressed.

1603-25

1610

1669

1680

1702

1770-80

1775-85

1795-99

1820

1803

1848

1860-70

1880-90

1885-95

1890's

1905

Hair styles of the **Twentieth Century** will be discussed in shorter periods.

Through the **First World War** the heavy look of teased women's hair was fading in favour of a more natural shape, with hair lapping over the ears into soft coils. During the War years the wide look quickly disappeared and hair just swept back and up onto the crown. Men continued the shaped look and were heavily influenced by the Military Cut.

1917-25

The Twenties introduced women to the bob, the shingle and the very sleek flat permanent wave. Flattened curls were used on the cheeks and forehead. Men, still with short hair, simply combed or slicked it back, fashionably clean shaven.

1920's

With **The Thirties** women favored the longer bob and the finger wave. Hair was brushed into soft waves, away from the face with a side part. Men were still influenced by the Military Cut but hair was growing out.

1930's

In **The Forties** the movies heavily influenced women's hair styles. Check those old movie magazines for the best reference. Men's style was combed back and soft but by mid-decade we were back to the Military Cut.

1937-45

The Fifties had the emergence of women's products - colour, wigs, perms, curls and short lived styles. The pony tail was youth and short; Butch, Urchin and Gamin cuts came and went. Men let their hair grow long, in the front, brushed or combed it high and back; of course, thinning hair meant combing it forward to cover.

1951-53

1955-59

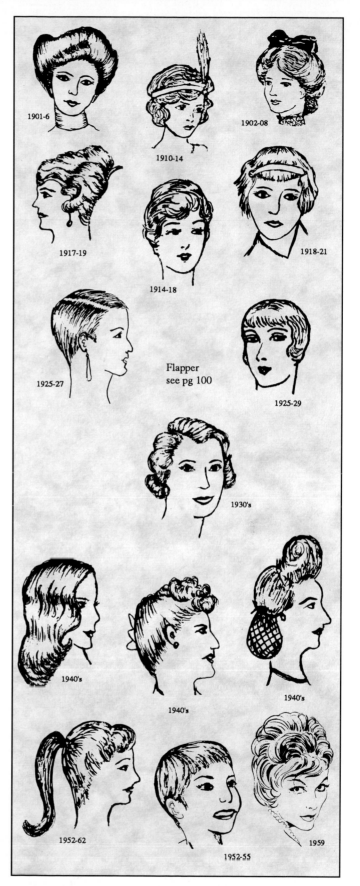

1901-6

1910-14

1902-08

1917-19

1914-18

1918-21

1925-27

Flapper see pg 100

1925-29

1930's

1940's

1940's

1940's

1952-62

1952-55

1959

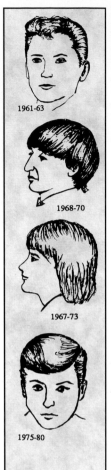

The **Sixties** saw the women's short hair fade and fad brought bouffant styles. Hair was piled high, beehived, knotted and lacquered into place. All of a sudden there were mountains of false pieces, falls, half and full wigs. False eyelashes were now the rage. Young Men's hair was falling forward and then came the Beatles.

The **Seventies** saw false hair fading and women's styles becoming wider and even nostalgic. Men's hair started getting long all over.

By **The Eighties** women were letting their natural lifestyles govern choice of hair style. Hot curlers made instant changes. Men were trimming back, although long hair stayed for some.

The last decade, **The Nineties**, seems to be more of that quick and casual. Men and women cutting hair to run a brush or comb and go.

(From the Twenties on, magazines are better references.)

Making the face look older

On the following pages we introduce a process of Old Age Make-Up. We have chosen the faces of both a young man and a young woman to illustrate the general techniques of applying the make-up. There are differences in the characteristics of aging that effect a man and a woman. It is important that you study the female as well as the male face.

Before you apply the make-up, take some time to study and understand the concepts of aging and the techniques of recreating age through make-up.

Aging starts at birth and gradually advances: the first two decades are primarily growth and adulthood, usually termed as *youth*; twenty to thirty-five are *mature*; thirty-five to sixty as *middle-age*; sixty to seventy-five *old age*; seventy to eighty-five *very old age*; and beyond eighty-five as *extreme old age*. Where any one person actually fits into a category depends on their genetic background, frame of mind, diet, and the care each has given their body.

There are many indications of advancing years. The most prominent are the loss of skin suppleness, the flesh becoming less firm, the bone structure becoming more apparent, the loss of youthful sheen to the skin and hair, and the increase of shadows and lines forming around the eyes, mouth and jaw. There are other important factors such as weight, height, natural colour of skin and hair.

Subtle changes in age are the most difficult to achieve. Advancing five to ten years, depending on the face and physique, may create the most complicated circumstances. Always remember that the intensity of stage light floods the face with light and washes the normal facial lines possibly reducing your onstage age. The direction of the light will also be a matter of consideration as to whether it will help or hinder your onstage aging process (see p. 13 Lighting). To reach your own age or the appearance of any particular age may require varying degrees of age make-up.

Generally, an increase in gray hair, more conservative hair style, higher temples, and less colour to skin will subtly advance a man's years. Hair style, a touch of crow's feet (lines) around the eyes, thinner lips and conservative costume dress will do the same for a woman. The addition of glasses or the occasional need to use them will help a great deal to imply added years.

Aging is also different depending on the character: Fat or thin, happy or sad, energetic, depressed, mean, nice, etc. The best way to study these differences is to collect photographs of different people at different ages. Several in each category will help build a stronger reference.

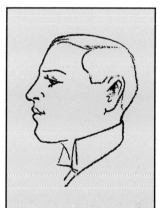

Full head of hair is an obvious sign of youth

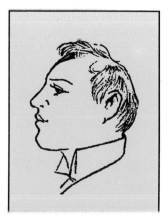

Padded Wig

Receded hairline quickly adds age to a man.

In older faces the expressive lines of the face become fixed as the muscles sag, and the skin hangs more loosely round the skull because the tissue has less body. Faces age very gradually and this should be taken into account when doing the make-up. A ten year difference between an actor and the part he is playing does not require a great deal of shadowing or highlighting.

Older faces depend particularly on contrasts. Make a note of the faces around you and the way in which they differ according to age. Age does not always mean deep folds and sunken cheeks.

Some of the ways in which faces change and which can be important in make-up are listed below. Depending on the results and/or age required, these can include:

- temples
- contours of the forehead
- lumps on the forehead
- folds at the bridge of the nose
- inner corner of the eye
- upper eyelid
- outer corner of the eye
- folds under the eye
- folds round the nose and lips
- cheekbones
- corners of the mouth
- chin
- folds in the neck
- line of the jaw
- neck

1

Ad's normal appearance. Take a good look at his face. Where are the contours and the folds in this face?

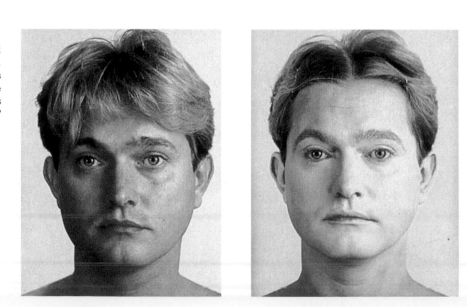

2

The foundation is a light ivory coloured greasepaint. The circulation in older skin is poorer, so that it often has a lighter, washed-out look.

3
Dark brown make-up is applied with a brush in places where shadows are required.

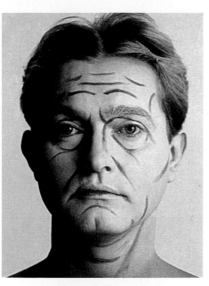

4
This brown make-up is blended into the foundation using a fingertip.

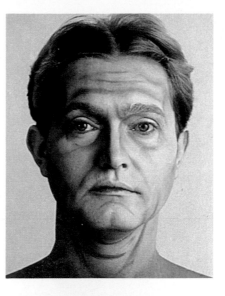

5
A very light coloured make-up is now applied next to all the shadows. Make a good note where the contours come with regard to these shadows.

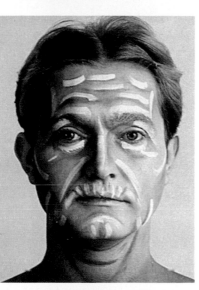

6
The highlights are also blended with the foundation and the shadowing. Make sure there are no stripes, only narrow patches of make-up. The make-up is then powdered.

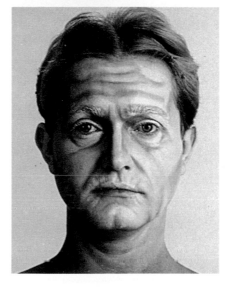

7
Using the fine grained sponge, lightly put some dark brown pancake onto the beard area. Make a parting in the hair and apply ivory coloured pancake with a sponge from the parting to either side of the hair. Then comb out the hair and spray on some hairspray.

Make sure the neck is also made up. An 'old' face on a young neck looks odd.

When making up an older person remember that age is not only portrayed with lines but also with a heightened contrast of light and dark. This applies to both men and women. Other details such as hair and clothes also contribute a great deal to the final result. In some cases it may be better to emphasize the age by the character's hair and clothes rather than by using too much make-up. Be careful not to fall into the trap of caricature, and always bear in mind the fashions of the time, the age of the character, and suitable clothes.

1 Nicole without make-up.

2 The hair is put up and a light ivory coloured foundation is applied. Blend carefully into the neck and hairline.

3
Depending on the natural contours and latent creases in the face, use a brush to apply shadows in those places.

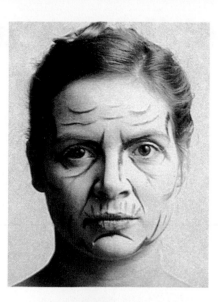

4
With the finger, blend the make-up into the foundation. Bear in mind which shadows need sharp edges, such as the fold under the eye and at the base of the nose.

5
Highlights are then applied against these dark shadows on the side where the contours are to come.

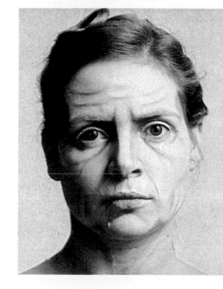

6
The light colour is blended into the foundation and with the shadows in those places where there are no sharp contours between light and dark. Then thoroughly powder the face and neck.

7
Using a fine grained sponge, pat some carmine red make-up on the cheek in a triangle along the fold of the nose and lips and under the cheekbone. Make sure that this does not go too high on the cheekbone, and do not apply the make-up too thickly.

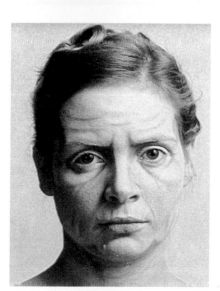

8
Put on a stocking cap and then put the wig on over this.

Make-up for children and fairytale characters

The make-up for a children's pantomime requires a great deal of imagination. It is often better to work with the suggestion of an idea or with stylised faces than to try to make the make-up seem as realistic as possible. Children playing children look better without make-up. Simply apply some rouge and emphasize the lips and eyes. If a foundation is required, use a light, fresh pink colour. To make children look older, use lines and wrinkles as little as possible and work with patches of colour. Grey hair or a wig, a pair of glasses, a moustache and/or a beard and the appropriate clothes will be more effective than a child's face elaborately made up to look old.

Flowers

This is a fantasy make-up in flowers and green. Again all sorts of variations using different shapes and colours are possible, but the techniques and procedures used always remain the same.

1
Scarlet without make-up.

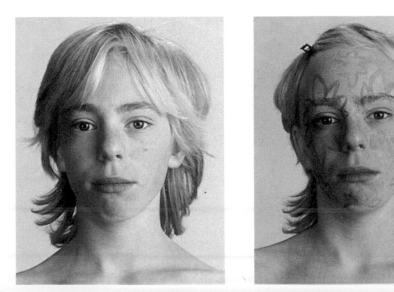

2
Using a thin brush (no. 6 or 8), the basic pattern is drawn onto the face in green greasepaint. The flowers should not be too close together, especially at the bridge of the nose.

3

The flowers are now filled in round the eyes and on the chin with white greasepaint. A circle round the eyes is left open so that the centre of the flower can be filled in later.

4

Now red flowers are filled in on the forehead and on the lower cheeks.

5

Using a grass green pancake, the rest of the face is filled in. The flowers can now be given a definite outline by making sure the eyes are very exact. The green make-up should go right up to the white or red flowers, leaving no strip of uncoloured skin, as this would mean that the patterns were no longer distinct.

6

The centres of the flowers are filled in with yellow greasepaint. The lips are also coloured yellow. Using a very fine brush and some green make-up, the veins of the leaves are drawn in.

7

The fantasy figure is completed with a wig made of gold foil purchased from a novelty shop, and some green gauze.

8

The same make-up has a different effect when it is set off against artificial grass and flowers.

Doll

The character of a doll or similar figure is quite common in children's theatre. Parts of this make-up can also be used for other figures in children's pantomimes; for example, the last photograph shows the same make-up with two extra lines to represent a ventriloquist's dummy.

1
Anouk without make-up.

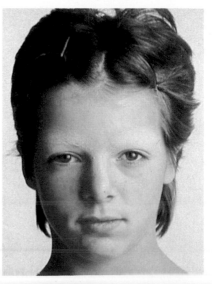

2
The eyebrows are brushed flat against the skin with a piece of toilet soap. When this is dry a layer of pancake can be patted over it.

3

The hard pink pancake is now evenly applied over the whole face.

4

A pearly silver blue greasepaint is applied on the upper eyelids from the eyelashes to just above the place where the eyebrows have been soaped. A circle of rouge (red greasepaint) is applied high up on the cheeks. Keep the round shape but slightly blur the edges.

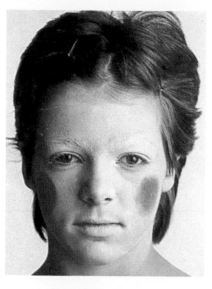

5

Using black pancake or a liquid eyeliner, draw in arched eyebrows above the eyeshadow. Also draw in the lower eyelashes. First draw the eyeliner along the edge of the eyelashes and then draw in vertical stripes. Both the eyebrows and the eyelashes can be drawn in first with a black pencil to prevent mistakes.

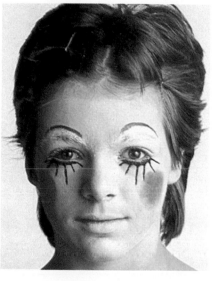

6

Large false eyelashes are now stuck to the upper eyelid. A small heart-shaped mouth is outlined and then filled in with the same red make-up as the rouge.

7

The doll is completed with a curly wig with small plaits, which can be bought ready-made Obviously lots of variations are possible here, e.g., using a woollen wig etc.

8

The same make-up used with a home-made wig and two vertical pencil lines drawn from the corners of the mouth downwards, give the impression of a ventriloquist's dummy.

Fairy

1

Karin without make-up.

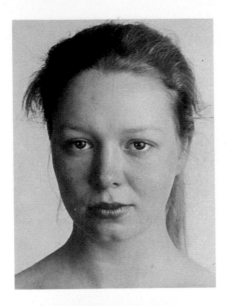

2

A light coloured pink pancake is applied thinly and evenly over the entire face.

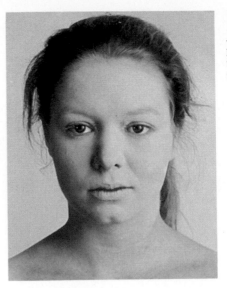

3

White pearly greasepaint is applied to the upper eyelids as far as the eyebrows. On top of this some silver glitter gel is dusted. Silver greasepaint is also used to draw the outlines of an eyebrow over the natural eyebrow and just above it.

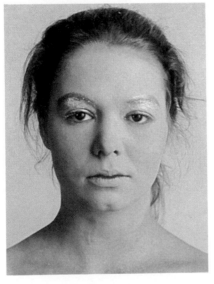

4

A little mauve glitter is used on top of the silver glitter. A thin brush is used to apply a pearly blue eyeliner. This is again covered with blue glitter. A little red glitter is used on the rouge on the cheeks, and the lips are filled in with a bright red colour.

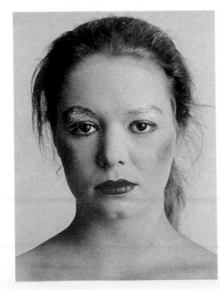

5

The whole face is powdered with silver glitter powder. The make-up is completed with a curly pink wig and a length of gauze.

Puss-in-Boots

1

An example of a stylised animal face. It can be used as a basis for many other animal faces.

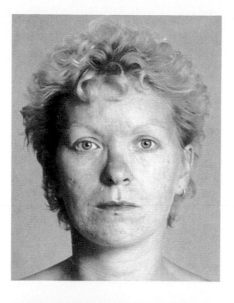

2

Using a black dermatographic pencil, draw the lines on the face, making a careful note of the black and white contrasts.

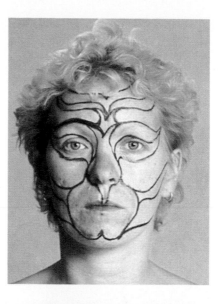

3

The spaces are filled in with white pancake. They have to be sharply outlined immediately.

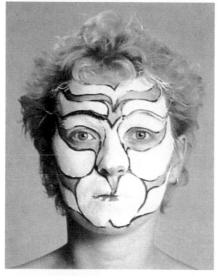

4

Now the remaining spaces are filled in with black pancake. The lines dividing the black and white areas should be very sharply drawn.

5

Using a thin brush the thin black lines are also drawn again and any unevennesses can now be corrected. The spots are drawn in on the upper lip, and the tip of the nose is coloured orangey-brown.

6

Depending on the costume to be worn, the throat and neck area are also made up. The head and ears are covered with a tightly wound white cloth. The head and the rest of the costume can be chosen according to the character's taste and insight.

Gnome

A gnome is an imaginary figure and everyone has his own idea of what a gnome looks like. The character chosen here is a rather carica-turised cartoon figure which can then be modified to a more natural look.

However, all the techniques needed for any type of gnome are included in this description.

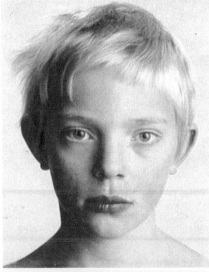

1
Rafael without make-up.

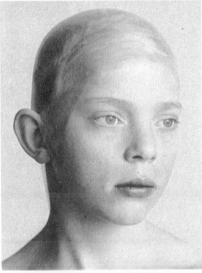

2
A glatzan skull cap is made to size and stuck down. At the same time the eyebrows are soaped.

3

A pinkish brown pancake is applied over the whole face and the glatzan.

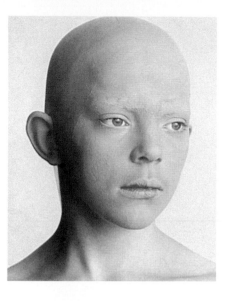

4

Using white crêpe hair, a complete fringe beard is stuck down from the top of the ears.

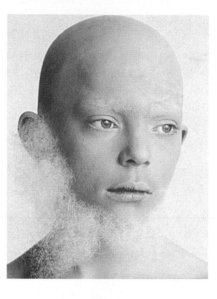

5

When the whole beard and moustache have been stuck down, they are carefully cut into a full round shape, as is the moustache.

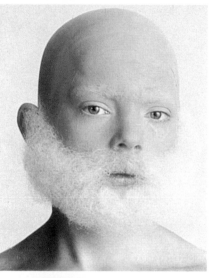

6

Shadows are applied on either side of the base of the nose, and dark make-up is used to draw a round fold from either side of the nose, just above the beard. Light coloured greasepaint is applied on the middle of the nose and along the rounded fold.

7

When this light make-up has been blended into the foundation, a fine grained sponge is used to apply medium red make-up along the fold and on the tip of the nose. A thin layer of red make-up is also applied to the lips. Using a black dermatographic pencil, thin rounded eyebrows are drawn in above the natural eyebrows.

8

The make-up can now be completed with white crêpe hair up to the edge of the hair, over the ears and on the back of the head. By adding eyebrows and a tuft of hair in the middle of the front of the glatzan, a completely different gnome can be created. The moustache is parted in the centre and the points are turned up. In addition, the folds under the eyes are slightly emphasized with dark and light make-up.

Witch

You can really go to town when making up as a witch. Nose putty, crêpe hair etc. can all be used to the full. To find out more about this, read the preceding sections on nose putty and crêpe hair.

1

Armanda without make-up.

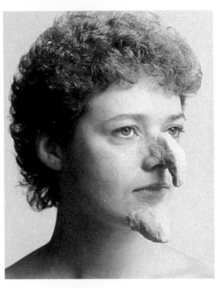

2

The nose and chin are made from nose putty and stuck onto the face.

See p 22, 23 and 25.

3

When the nose putty has been fixed so that it joins smoothly onto the skin, a thin layer of beige greasepaint is applied to the face and over the nose putty. This should be done very carefully so that the nose putty is not moved.

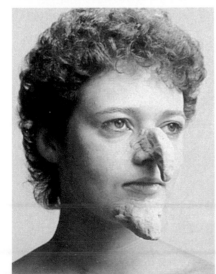

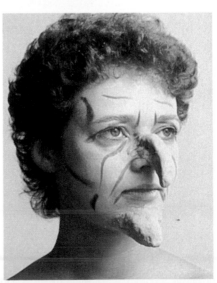

4

Using a brush and dark brown greasepaint some lines are drawn on the face. These lines are used to produce a sharp and rather thin impression.

5

The lines are merged into the foundation with the finger, though without totally losing their effect.

6

Very light highlights are applied against the shadows.

7

When this colour has also been blended in with the finger, a fine grained sponge is used to put carmine red make-up over the entire face. Some of this red make-up is also applied under the lower eyelid and on the warts on the nose and chin. (These are made from nose putty rolled into balls and pressed onto the nose and chin.) Some more dark grey make-up is patted on the lower cheeks and on the sides of the nose and chin.

8

Using grey crêpe hair, eyebrows are stuck down just above the natural eyebrows. Grey make-up is applied to the lips without using any contrast, making sure that the corners of the mouth turn downwards.

9

The make-up is completed with a home-made wig of hemp dyed a dirty grey colour and sewn in the middle onto a piece of cloth. Muss the hair, then style it so that it becomes rather peaky. The cloth is attached to the hair with hairgrips.

10

Finally the witch wears a pointed black cardboard hat covered with black material, a loose piece of gauze and a thick black wrap.

Animal make-up

To incorporate the features of an animal onto a face, or to transfer the characteristics of an animal's head for visual characterisation, requires technical expertise as well as insight. It is best to start by looking for drawings of the animal that has been modelled on nature as closely as possible.

On this drawing find the lines which show perspective and places where shadows or highlights are used on the head. Now transfer these basic lines onto the drawing of a face. Using this technique you can then elaborate the make-up for the face as you apply it. Save your sketches for reference and update as you modify the facial design.

Animal character make-up can be extremely elaborate or just suggestive. It is all important that you maintain a familiarity with the animal's features, movements and habits. The costume you use will often add much to the believability of the character. But, the facial design is of primary importance. Make-up that allows the audience to accept the performer as an animal and still allows the performer the flexibility of facial movement is always most desirable. The performer's features are enlarged, not obscured, and facial communication is intensified.

The effect is complete, only when the performer captures the vitality, warmth and gesticulation of the animal.

To assist in creating animal faces there are many flexible prosthetic pieces that can be used for noses, mouths, ears, jaws, etc. Be careful not to select a piece that inhibits your creation. Some of the most effective animal faces are the simplest and my reference to rubber pieces is to show availability. I personally prefer to work with the face and make-up.

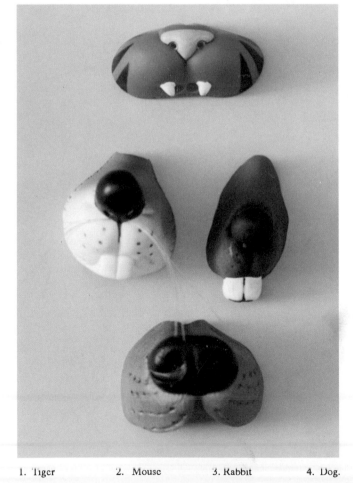

1. Tiger   2. Mouse   3. Rabbit   4. Dog.

THE WIZARD OF OZ, A WONDRAWHOPPER by William-Alan Landes, is a marvelous example of animal and fantasy characters. (Jim Slaughter, Kathy O'Connel, Ronald Waldron, Marjorie E. Clapper, Don Agey.)

Animal

1

2

Sketch eyelines, nose and upper lip shapes with Black make-up.

3

Highlight around dark shapes with a light colour.

5

Accent hair with spray colours. We styled the model's natural hair into "ear" shapes and streaked it with Silver and White spray.

4

Accent remaining areas with a colour of your choice (we used Silver).

Make-up by Joe Rossi & Company.
Courtesy of Mehron, Inc.

Cat

Cats or members of the cat family occur in fairytales and children's pantomimes, but are very suitable for a carnival or a fancy dress party.

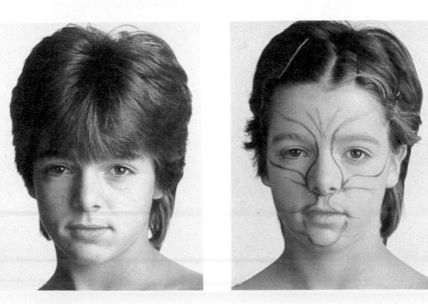

1 Anouk without make-up.

2 A yellowish brown foundation (pancake) is applied evenly. Using a dark brown greasepaint the basic outlines are now drawn in with a thin brush.

3

When these dark brown lines have been merged with the foundation, light coloured beige highlights are applied next to the shadowed areas.

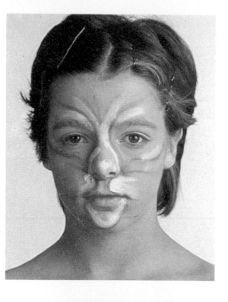

4

This light coloured make-up is also blended in. Some dark brown make-up is now applied in bold lines on the upper eyelid and along the lower eyelid. These lines end in a point downwards at the nose, and upwards at the outer corners of the eyes. Additional shadows are put in along the light make-up on either side of the nose and chin.

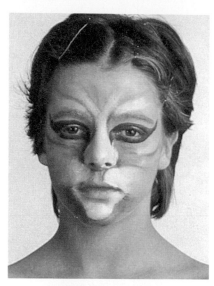

5

Using a thin brush (no. 6 or 8, or an eyeliner brush), draw in short stripes of dark brown greasepaint over the entire make-up, except on the tip of the nose, the upper lip and the centre of the chin. Make sure that the direction of the stripes is from the tip of the nose radiating outwards in every direction. The tip of the nose is darker, turning into stripes on the upper lip. The lips should also be dark and pointing downwards.

6

Now very light stripes are drawn in between the dark stripes in the same way.

7

Using yellow greasepaint, a few more stripes are put in between those already there. A light brown stripe is drawn in above the dark make-up on the tip of the nose. Dots are drawn in with the point of a brush on either side of the stripes on the upper lip.

8

The make-up is completed by a small fur cap with ears. This cap can also be made from lining silk; the lines on the face should continue onto the cap.

Dog

1

When making up a dog, the general characteristics which distinguish dogs from other animals should be taken into account, rather than the specific breed. Not all characteristics of a particular breed can be shown on the face, and these characteristics are better shown by the use of colour than by line. Armanda without make-up.

2

The glatzan should be cut to size and stuck down. Then the basic lines are applied with dark brown pancake. These lines run from the middle of the face down and outwards.

3

The spaces between the lines are filled in with reddish brown and yellowish brown pancake.

4

The lines and the spaces are slightly blended into each other with a clean, damp brush. Some more light coloured make-up is applied over the eyebrows, on the nose and on the upper lip. Black make-up is applied to the tip of the nose, a line from the nose to the middle of the upper lip and the lips, and black dots are painted above the upper lip. Some light highlights are applied from the middle line of the face.

5

Two floppy ears are cut from foam rubber, painted dark brown and stuck against the side of the head with mastic. A hairy imitation fur suit completes the costume.

Panther

1
Nicole without make-up.

2
A yellowish brown pancake foundation is evenly applied over the entire face.

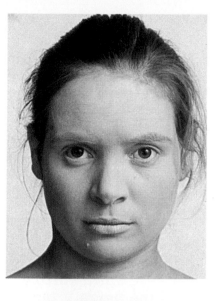

3
The basic lines for the make-up are drawn in with a wide brush and dark brown face paints. These are then blended into the foundation with the finger.

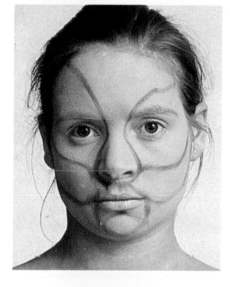

4
A yellowish white make-up is then applied next to these dark lines and blended into the foundation with the finger in the same way. The nose, chin and upper lip should be particularly strongly highlighted.

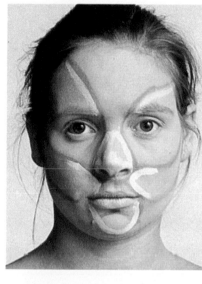

5
With a narrow brush the eyes can be outlined with a wide line of dark brown pancake so that the inside corners point downwards while the outside corners point upwards. Next, the panther spots are applied arbitrarily, but radiating outwards from the nose in a star shape. Apply dark brown make-up to the mouth so that the corners of the mouth are pointing down. Draw a vertical line from the nostrils to the middle of the upper lip and put in a few dark brown dots on either side.

6
A fake fur cap is made up with the same sort of pattern and worn as a wig over the ears. The rest of the costume is also painted in a panther pattern.

Mouse

The cat's great partner in many cartoons, comic strips, children's books and pantomimes is the mouse. Apart from the traditional grey mouse described below, there are a number of well-known caricatures such as Mickey Mouse, and Jerry (of Tom and Jerry). It is also possible to do make-up for these characters, and when doing this remember the characteristics from the pictures; for example, Mickey Mouse's big, round black nose.

To make up a mouse the use of lines is very important for effective results. On the other hand, there are a number of characteristic features in a mouse's head which will contribute to the success of the figure if they are carefully applied, such as the pointed face – at least in the familiar town mouse – the large ears and eyes, the divided upper lip and the two large incisors. The mouse is usually portrayed in grey. When the costume is made, don't forget the long segmented tail, which should be as long as the rest of the body.

1

Scarlet without make-up.

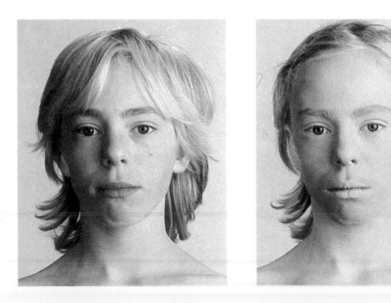

2

A grey pancake is applied evenly over the entire face. Remember that thicker areas of make-up will result in visible patchiness.

3

The basic lines are drawn in with a narrow brush and dark grey greasepaint. These run from the tip of the nose and the upper lip outwards in a star shape.

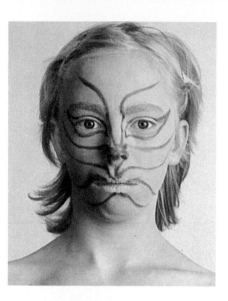

4

These dark lines are now blended into the foundation with the finger, and a triangle on the chin is coloured completely dark grey. A wide outline of dark grey make-up is applied to the eyes, pointing down at the inside corner of the eye and up at the outside corners. The tip of the nose is coloured dark grey, as are the lips.

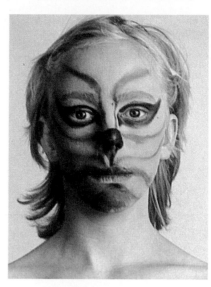

5

A very light greasepaint is applied next to the dark areas with a brush.

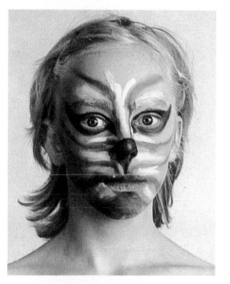

6

This light make-up is blended into the foundation with the finger.

7

Using a very fine brush some small thin, almost white stripes are drawn in in the same star-shaped pattern as the dark areas. A few long dark lines are drawn on the upper lip to represent whiskers. The two incisors are outlined on the lower lip with a black pencil and filled in with white make-up.

8

A small cap with two pointed ears is made from lining silk; a piece of grey lining silk has been folded round the model in this picture as a suggestion for the costume.

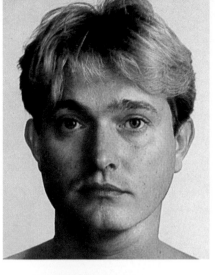

1
Ad without make-up.

Lion

This make-up is a combination of the most natural possible look and a stylised image. The most important feature is the sisal hair-piece which completes the picture.

2
A yellowish brown pancake foundation is applied with a sponge.

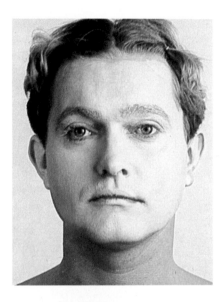

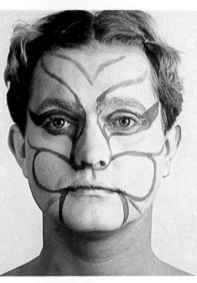

3
The basic pattern is drawn in with dark brown make-up.

4
The dark brown make-up is spread over particular areas, such as the bottom of the face and along the wide nose.

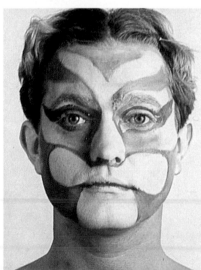

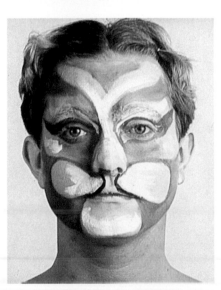

5
A light coloured make-up is applied inside and next to the dark areas.

6
This is blended into the foundation while the contrast in colour is maintained. The tip of the nose and the middle of the upper lip are coloured black. The lower eyelid is outlined in black, pointing downwards at the inner corner of the eye and upwards at the outer corner.

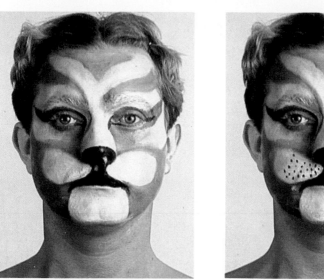

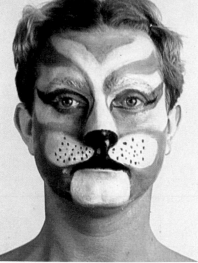

7
Black dots are filled in on the upper lip and some of the contrasts can now be toned down.

8
A sisal hairpiece with two ears is put on, surrounding the whole face. First put on one part as a beard, and then put on the other part as a wig.

Character make-up

Through the ages various characters have assumed more or less fixed images. Obviously a personal interpretation of these characters is always brought in, but the basis remains the same. In this section a few of these characters are described, though they may also be found in other sections.

Tramp
This make-up can also be used to portray a wanderer or a down-and-out character.

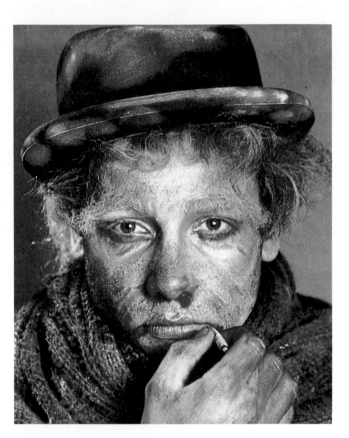

Martin without make-up.

2 A rather pale greyish beige shade of foundation is applied to the face, also covering the eyebrows.

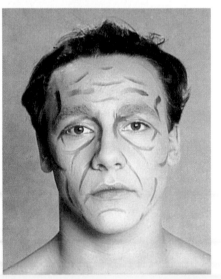

3 A dark greenish-brown make-up is used to draw in the shadows. These are applied on those parts where the structure of the face can be used to create a deeply lined look. The make-up is then blended into the foundation with the finger.

4

A light coloured make-up is applied with a brush adjacent to the shadowy areas. The position of the light colour next to the shadow depends on the contours required. Examine photographs 3 and 4 to find out where these contours will be.

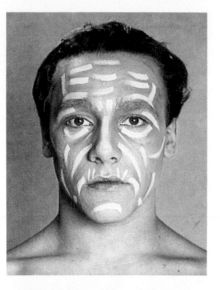

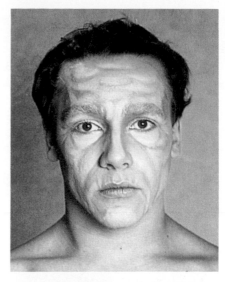

5

Blend the lines of light make-up into the foundation and with the shadows. In some places, such as in the wrinkles on the forehead, the line between light and dark can be quite sharp, while the light and dark make-up should blend together evenly in other places such as on the temples and the cheeks. A stronger colour emphasis is also required in some places to suggest raised contours.

6

For the stubble, first prepare those parts of the face where there would be a natural beard growth with a thick stubble paste stick. A powder brush is then used to apply extremely small pieces of crêpe hair over this area. Make sure that the crêpe is applied evenly.

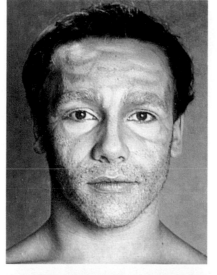

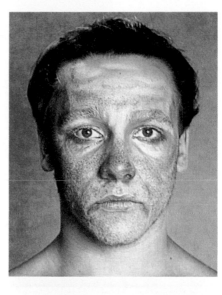

7

Carmine coloured make-up is dabbed onto the face with a fine grained sponge, especially on the cheeks and nose. This red make-up is also applied to the eyelids under the lower eyelashes, using a fine brush.

8

Grey crêpe eyebrows are stuck down immediately above the natural eyebrows and are then cut into shape.

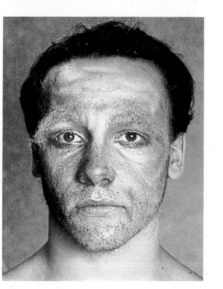

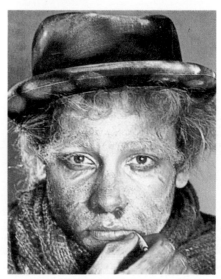

9

The hair is slightly curled and dyed grey with off-white make-up. It is then mussed in all directions. Make sure that the hands are also made up. Black fingernails would be a feature of this make-up.

Skull

Skulls and related figures, such as the allegorical grim reaper, occur in various plays and other depictions. There is an essential difference between a skull and Death. The first is a real object for which an anatomical knowledge of the skull is required. On the other hand, Death would be an imaginary figure which can be interpreted in an individual way and may have all sorts of shapes and colours. To portray this, use the shadows and dark areas of the skull, but do not make them quite as clear and distinct. Keep the features vague. It may not even be necessary to use a bald head. This could be replaced by plastered down hair or a wide cape.

1

Armanda without make-up.

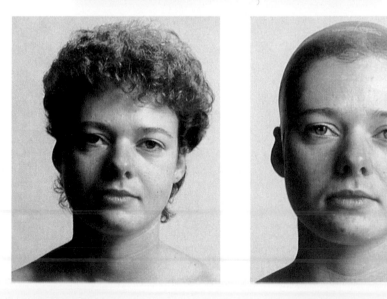

2

A glatzan is cut to size and stuck down. In this example the ears have been cut free, but if the skull appears without any covering or cape, do not cut out the ears – leave them under the glatzan.
A small round hole can then be cut at the level of the ear so that hearing is not impaired.

3

Using an ivory coloured foundation make up the face and the glatzan in two layers. The first layer is brushed on; the second is patted on. Make sure that the transition from the skin to the glatzan is well covered with make-up.

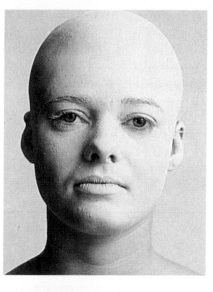

4

Using a black pencil, draw in the basic lines around the eyes, the tip of the nose and the mouth.

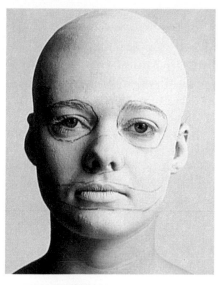

5

Fill in these spaces around the eyes and the tip of the nose with black pancake. With a thin brush draw in the pencil lines of the teeth. Make sure that these are not too regular and remember the difference in the width of the upper and lower teeth and between the front teeth and the back molars.

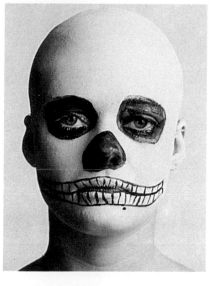

6

The spaces for the teeth are now filled in with white make-up. Grey and white grease paint is used to suggest an effect of depth in some parts of the make-up, e.g., on the forehead, cheekbones and temples, eyebrow arches and chin. To do this, consult a drawing of a skull.

7

A black cloth is tightly wound round the head so that the top of the skull is clearly visible.

8

A joke face.

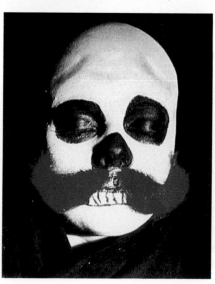

Punk

'Punk' is the well-known youth culture which became popular at the end of the 1970s. This makes it the natural successor of the beatniks of the 1950s, the rock culture of the 1960s and the hippy movement which followed this.

The characteristic features of the punk movement include the shrill music and coarse lyrics of the songs, as well as the style or dress of punks.

Bright colours are used in profusion, both in the hairstyles, which often consist of spiky cuts, and in the make-up, which is often very bizarre. The accompanying clothing is usually rather ragged and bedecked with punk ornamentation such as safety pins, razor blades and heavy chains.

However, punks are very individual with regard to their appearance. In making up a punk image this also depends to a large extent on the personal interpretation of this phenomenon. In the example shown here we have chosen a Mohican with a rather aggressive look.

1

Peter without make-up.

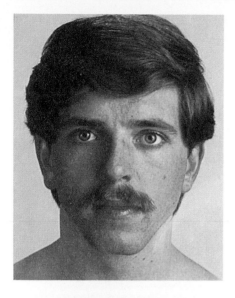

2

Using black pancake draw the stylised unbroken eyebrows with a brush without using any foundation.

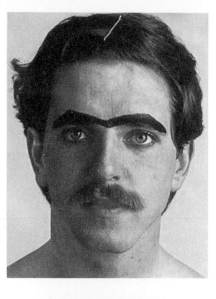

3

Lines are drawn down from the eyebrows along the nose. The lower eyelids are outlined with two thick lines.

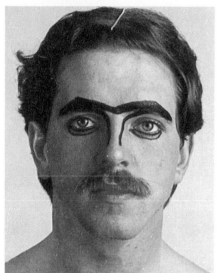

4

An asymmetric basic pattern is drawn on the cheeks in black. On one side there is a flash of lightning; on the other side, a triangle.

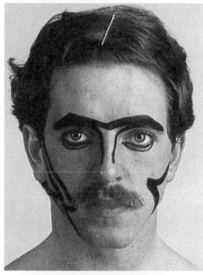

5

Shiny silver make-up is applied to the bridge of the nose and next to the black patterns on the cheeks. Red make-up is drawn between the black lines under the eyes and between the black lines of the flash of lightning.

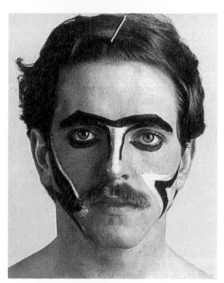

6

The model's moustache has been coloured a deep black. A bright green line is drawn over the eyebrows. A rubber cap with a brightly coloured Mohican is worn. The cap in the example is not made up and a stronger impression is thus created, but obviously it can be made up in the same colours and/ or patterns as the skin.

Pirate

1

Luppo without make-up.

2

A dark reddish brown foundation is unevenly applied over the face and neck.

3

Shadows are applied to the temples, forehead, folds under the eyes, between the nose and lips and at the corners of the mouth, with dark brown make-up. Be careful with the shadows on the nose. Draw a wavy line the length of the nose from the bridge down to the tip. When this is highlighted it gives an impression of a broken nose.

4

Highlights are drawn in next to all the shadows, again paying particular attention to the line down the nose. The light coloured make-up is carefully blended into the foundation with the finger.

5

Draw a scar on the cheek. With a dark brown pencil put in the line. Next to this, draw a light coloured line and then another line of carmine red make-up. The stitch marks are drawn with a brown pencil and for every mark add a little line of light make-up on one side. This makes a fairly old scar, but when the carmine red is replaced by bright blood red, the scar looks more recent.

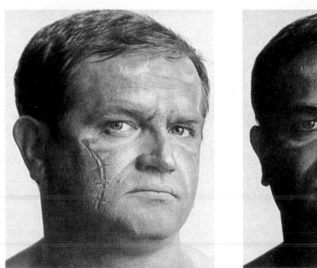

6

The eyes are outlined with black pencil, and the eyebrows are also emphasized with this. More shadows are drawn in on the sockets of the eye and the lips are coloured orangey brown.

76

7

A dark brown beard is made with crêpe hair. This should not be too long, but should be quite full; stick down the crêpe from the chin and work upwards to the ears.

8

At the place where the beard joins the hairline at the sideburns, it should be cut shorter.
The rest of the beard may look rather unkempt, but it should not be uneven. Dab the whole face with a fine grained sponge with red make-up, putting a little extra round the nose and on the cheeks.

9

A rather ragged moustache of short crêpe hair is stuck down. This can be quite thin and should run down the fold between the nose and lips to join with the beard.

10

Using the same crêpe hair, stick some hair on the chest. The look is completed with an eye patch and a scarf knotted round the head. It can be knotted either at the side or at the back.

Devil or Dracula

The Dracula figure made up here is based on a long tradition. The combination of animal and human features is derived from early representations of the devil. In medieval art great use was made of animal figures such as the snake, the boar (teeth), the goat (hooves and horns), the vulture and the bat (cape). At a later date these animal figures acquired a human head and some of the features became increasingly stylised. The examples below show these stylised versions. The figure of the devil is always a great success at a carnival and everybody knows the horror story of Count Dracula, who lives in a castle in a remote area of Eastern Europe and terrorises the region with his nightly searches for human blood.

Be careful with the use of lines in this make-up. The basic Dracula lines can also be used for a Mephistopholes creation (without the teeth and with a pointed beard and moustache).

The false teeth with the two fangs are available from novelty shops, and create the Dracula effect.

A narrow moustache of black crêpe hair is stuck down, leaving a wide gap in the middle; it does not extend beyond the corners of the mouth.

1

Paul without make-up.

2

A yellowish brown foundation is applied evenly to the face.

3

When the eyebrows have been outlined, they are filled in with black pancake.

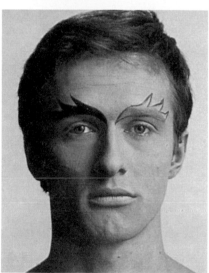

4

Using a fine brush, apply a reddish brown make-up to places where shadows or character lines are required. The lines on the forehead run more or less parallel to the eyebrows.

5

These lines are blended into the foundation with the finger.

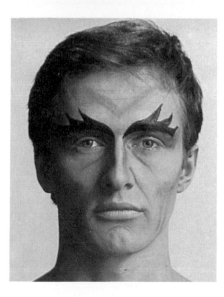

6

A whitish beige make-up is applied next to these shadowed areas, taking into account the contrast between the light and dark make-up.

7

Again the light coloured make-up is blended with the shadowy areas into the foundation with the finger.

8

The eyes are boldly outlined with black liquid eyeliner, pointing down at the inner corner of the eye and up at the outer corner. The upper lip is sharply defined, especially in the middle, and the corners of the mouth are continued downwards. The fleshy side of the nostril is coloured black.

9

The hair is combed forwards into a point so that it follows the line of the shadows on the forehead.

10

A goatee of black crêpe hair is stuck down on the chin with a sharply defined join in a 'W' shape. A black devil's cap emphasizes the sinister look of this make-up.

11

The false teeth can now be put in the mouth. The shape of the teeth is followed with blood red make-up on the lower lip. Extra red make-up on the lips around the nose and below the eyeliner on the lower lip produce an even more bloodthirsty expression.

Werewolf

1

Apply a thin coat of spirit gum on area where modelling putty/wax will be applied. When nearly dry, sculpt desired nose shape.
HINT: Rough sculpt shapes and blend edges into skin. Lubricate fingers with Make-up Remover Cream to smooth shapes. Texture surface with stipple sponge.

2

Cover entire face and sculpted shapes with Base make-up and powder.

3

Create shadows with Brown make-up. The "hard edges" of shadow can be deepened with Black. Paint nose and upper lip line with Black.

Apply Crêpe Hair (see page 35)

4

Trim and Style the Crêpe Hair.

Make-up by Joe Rossi & Company.
Courtesy of Mehron, Inc.

Vampira

The female counterpart to Dracula. Again, you will find much of the concept coming from medieval art, combining animal features to the human form. The stylized Devil or Dracula, as depicted on page 78, gives way to a cinematic approach where the human features predominate but are amplified with a deathly look - *the living dead*.

Much of the technique is the same as on pages 79-80, with less emphasis on stylization and a predominance of the *horror* realistic. This concept, although depicted here for a woman, is just as applicable for a male vampire.

1

Apply a thin, even coat of a pale colour make-up. You may need to blend white or green into your base make-up to add that deathly effect. Lightly dust with translucent powder and remove excess with a powder brush.

2

Using Black make-up, *hollow* facial cavities to add angularity to the face. Darken the eyebrows, and add liner around the eyes. Depending on distance from the audience, and age of your character (see Making the face look older, pages 45-48) add appropriate depth of age make-up.

3

Paint mouth Red, as shown, or Black for a more ghastly effect.

4

Accentuate the temple area with Black make-up; for a more natural, close look, use crêpe hair. Gently powder fresh make-up areas and brush off excess with Powder Brush.

5

Draw in blood dripping from mouth with Red make-up.

6

Complete the look, add fangs dripped in stage blood and a wig. (The wig can be Black, Black and Grey, Grey streaked hair.) For a gruesome look use strange coloured hair. For a more natural look use your own hair and touch with grey or liquid white.

Courtesy of Dana Nye, Ben Nye Make-up.

Santa Claus
Father Christmas

This is another prototype. Anyone with a white beard and a red suit is Santa Claus, or Father Christmas, but because this character is mainly a figure for children, it is worth taking some extra care. In this way he can retain some of his magic, while a careless attempt would have a disillusioning effect.

1 Luppo without make-up.

2 A light pinkish-beige foundation is applied thinly and evenly with a damp sponge.

3

Dark brown make-up is applied with a fine brush to the parts of the face where folds and/or contours are required. Use the structure of the face that is being made up and adapt the shadows to this structure.

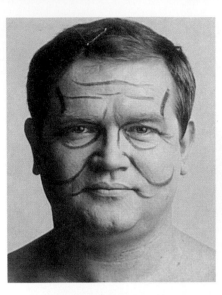

4

The dark make-up is blended into the foundation with the finger. Watch the colour contrasts in the various places.

5

Apply some whitish-beige highlights next to each shadow with a fine brush, making sure of the places where the contours are required in relation to the shadows. Highlights above or below produce horizontal shadows, and to the left or right, produce vertical shadows.

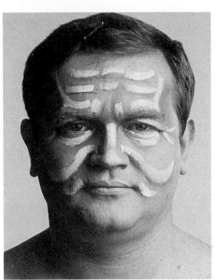

6

The light coloured make-up is then blended thoroughly into the foundation with the finger. Watch where bold or soft divisions are required between highlights.

7

The light coloured make-up is also applied to the eyebrows to highlight these. Using a fine grained sponge, dab some red make-up along the rounded fold between the nose and the lips, rounded to the side. This can be fairly heavy. Some of the make-up is also applied thinly to the tip of the nose and above the eyebrows.

8

The beard can now be put on. The elastic is held in the hair with a number of hairgrips on top of the head. Make sure that the beard is positioned centrally, and to be quite sure, the beard can be stuck onto the chin with mastic.

9

An edge of white crêpe hair can be stuck onto the skin along the hard edge of the beard. Make sure that the crêpe hair has been properly prepared and that there are no clumps.

10

When it has been stuck along the whole edge of the crêpe beard, it is pulled down between the hairs of the beard with the point of a pointed comb, ensuring a gradual transition.

11

White crêpe hair is also stuck down above the natural eyebrows. This should not be too wide and should be no longer than the natural eyebrows. When the tufts have been stuck down, they are pressed down as far as possible over the natural eyebrows.

12

The eyebrows are cut into shape, not too long and bushy.

13

The moustache is firmly stuck down. Apply one layer of mastic above the upper lip and leave to dry; then cover this with a second layer of mastic and immediately firmly press the moustache onto this and hold. If the top edge of the moustache is rather hard, some more crêpe hair can be stuck down above it and combed in.

14

Put on the wig and push back as far as possible so that some of the forehead is visible. Make sure that the wig lies flat against the skin on the sides so that there is no gap. If there is a gap, stick down the front of the wig to the skin.

Racial make-up

In order to create a successful racial type, the face should form the basis of the make-up and not the racial stereotype. Find out which are the characteristic lines of any particular racial type and then transfer these onto a European face. There are Chinese people with round faces as well as with long faces. Not all Red Indians have a hooked nose and not all Italians have black hair and a moustache. Similarly, not all Scandinavians have blond hair. Remember that in some cases the hair can contribute more to an image than a make-up which attempts to approximate reality in a caricatured way.

Europeans The European people are basically Caucasoids with the following variations:

Northern Europeans *(Dutch, Belgians, English, Scandinavians)*...use lighter tones.

Central and Eastern Europeans *(Austrians, the Czechoslovaks, the French from the central regions, the Swiss, those from the Balkans, Ukraine and Russia)* - use medium shades. For the Russians add a bit more red.

Mediterraneans *(Spanish, Portuguese, the French from the south of France, the Italians, Greeks, and some Irish and Welsh)* Use varying shades from amber to olive-beige. Remember to use darker tones when they are people exposed to a great deal of sunlight.

Asians There are many nationalities and races included in this area: Central Europeans, Russians, Spanish, Portuguese, Egyptians, Arabs (see page 92), Hebrews, Jews, Orientals. Most are of Mediterranean decent.

Southwestern Asians *(Arabs, Iranians, Persians, Hebrews)*
Your make-up should favour the beige and yellowish tones. Remember that these people have facial or body hair, which is usually very dark and fuzzy.
Iranians and Persians who are often decended from Mediterranean, Arab-Armenian or Mongoloid forebears should draw their shades from light brown colours.

South Asians *(East Indians)* These East Indian people are also derived from many races and their skin tones may vary considerably: pale brown-olive, light greyish brown, dark brown, chocolate brown, copperish brown, very light yellowish brown to a hazel-yellowish brown.

It is important to remember that the further away from China the less yellow in the skin colours.

Central Asians This area includes people from Tibet, Mongolia and part of Siberia. They have very little facial or body hair. The complexion tones range from very light brown to hazel-yellowish brown.

Ocean Islanders *(Australia, New Zealand, Melanesia, Polynesia, New Guinea, Tasmania, and Micronesia)* The territory that ranges from Australia to the Isle of Papua New Guinea, and from New Zealand to Hawaii. Australia and New Zealand have a great majority of their population from the Caucasoid race, mostly decendent from Northern Europeans (see Europeans). The aborigines are a chocolate brown with very curly black hair and heavy beards (Caucasoid and Negro combination).

Melanesian inhabitants have dark curly hair, very little on their face or body. Polynesians and Hawaiians have very dark hair, straight or slightly wavy. All of the island people have a dark olive to medium brown skin colour. The Melanesians and Papuans belong to the Australian-Aboriginal race that originally lived in Tasmania.

Micronesia includes the Marshall Islands, the Carolinas, the Mareannas and Gilbert Island. The people are of the Caucasoid-Negroid race, with skin tones of medium brown with slight yellow highlights. They generally have the black frizzy hair.

Americans

North Americans *(U.S.A., Canada, American Indian)* Most have the same characteristics as the European forebears except the American Indian (see page 96).

Central and South Americans *(Mayans, Incas, Yucatans, the Jivaro)* These people are all South American Indians. Their skin colours and features are similar to the North American Indians, except for their hair styles.

For the Mexicans and other South and Central Americans use shades with varying tones of olive or yellowish brown. Hair and eyes are very dark. If there is a strong Spanish decent then the skin colour is lighter and there will be more facial and body hair than the Mexican or Indian.

Greek, Roman *(Ancient)* The Greek and Roman of today is not the Classic Helenic. The men and women are noted for unusual handsomeness with sleek well defined physiques. The nose is straight and connects with the forehead in an almost unbroken line. The face is oval with well curved lips and prominent chin. The eyes are large and well

placed under classically curved brows. The complexion and hair are dark in tone with a blending of brown for a darker skin type. The lips should be painted in a clean-cut, classic curve. Outline the eyes in black, enlarging them as much as possible, darken the eye lashes. A dot of red on the inner corner will help enlarge the eye.

Egyptians *(Ancient)* The mighty Egyptian is depicted as preserved on monuments and tomb decorations: The aristocrat is tall, slender, with a noble and dignified carriage. he possessed broad shoulders, muscular limbs, slight hips and fine hands and feet. The face was shaped with even proportions in length and width. The nose straight or aquiline, eyes large and dark; the whole expression charming and proud. The peasants are shown with the same characteristics but of shorter stature.

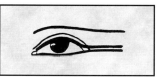

Egyptian style
Eye make-up.

The skin colour should be sunburnt brown with hints of dull yellow. Women can be much lighter in tone and should suggest red on the cheekbones. The elongated eye which we note from the Theban Monuments should be used for ladies of rank.

INDIAN TALES, stylized musical, by William-Alan Landes. (Roz Witt, Carlos Hernandez, Mike Kanopa.)

Far Easterner *(Chinese, Japanese)* Two distinct races are attributed to this area: One is tall, with very fine features, black hair and almond-shaped eyes but not of the Mongoloid type. The other is short and stocky, heavy bones, and jet black hair. The eyes are of the classic Mongoloid type and their skin is darker than the first group.

Both groups need the yellowish beige shades. Their facial hair is usually non-existant and both men and women age prematurely. The eyebrow does not have hair growing at the end thus creating the *wing* cut or *high arch*. The best ways to hide the Caucasian eyebrow are to soap out, cover with latex, or block out with make-up.

The Japanese race, called Ainu, is an ancient Caucasoid/Mongolian group and are different from the usual Japanese race. Their skin tones need a warm beige with bushy black hair and beard.

Differences to be noted, between Chinese and Japanese are: Chinese lips are usually fuller and coarser than those of the Japanese; faces are rounder for Chinese; Japanese have high cheekbones. The eyes vary significantly, some even have an almost Caucasian appearance; the Mongolians and the Manchus are not as oblique (slanted) as those of the true Chinese, and the Japanese, at least on stage, seem to emphasize the oblique slant.

Chinese

The colour of the skin is *not* lemon yellow, and this colour can only be used for a caricature or fantasy figure.

1

Ad without make-up.

2

A yellowish brown foundation slightly tinged with green is applied. This colour should be applied very thinly and evenly.

3

The shadows and highlights are applied in accordance with racial characteristics. On the forehead these areas run from the middle, slanting upwards. The upper eyelids are slightly highlighted. The cheekbones are also highlighted and some shadow is applied below them. The folds from the nose to the corner of the mouth, the upper lip and the chin are slightly emphasized.

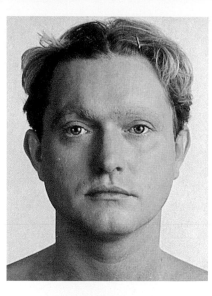

4

The eyebrows are drawn in at an angle with a black pencil. They should not be too long. Next, the eyes are outlined to determine the slant of the eyes. The outline of the eyes should be drawn slanting sharply downwards from the upper eyelids to the nose and upwards at the outer corners of the eyes. The lower line begins at the end of the top line of the nose and then runs parallel to the top line at the outer corners of the eyes.

5

A line of very light coloured make-up should be applied along the line above the eye, from the beginning of the nose to the middle of this line. The same colour should be applied between the two parallel lines at the outer corners of the eyes.

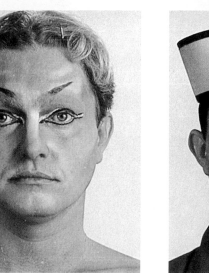

6

Colour in a small brownish red mouth and stick down the moustache made from uncurled crêpe or other hair, keeping a wide gap between the two sides. If no head covering is worn, a glatzan skull cap can be used with a pigtail made from a black nylon stocking stuck down on the crown of the head. The head-dress used in the example covers a black cloth bound tightly round the head; the hair showing underneath has been dyed black with pancake.

Geisha girl

The original meaning of the Japanese word 'geisha' is servant, but from the end of the eighteenth century the term has been used to refer to the Japanese hostesses whose function is to provide company for guests during a meal and to entertain them with dance, music and conversation. They also serve at table. Geisha girls undergo a long training to learn their profession and are contracted to geisha houses by their parents at a very young age. The make-up for a geisha girl is more or less fixed. It is important to emphasize her role as a servant, and this is done by hiding her individuality by the make-up. This 'closed' look of the face is typically Japanese. (There are also standard masks for some of the different theatrical roles.)

Nevertheless, it is always possible to incorporate small variations, particularly in the way the eyebrows are drawn. The classical Japanese make-up descibed here uses the motif of a butterfly. This motif recurs in the wig, the make-up – especially the mouth – and in the garment worn, the kimono.

1

Karin without
make-up.

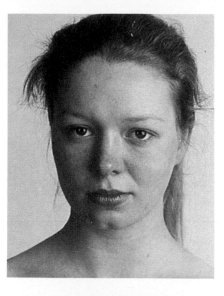

2

An off-white
foundation is applied
to the face in two
layers. The first layer
is brushed on and left
to dry; the second layer
is patted on. The
make-up should
continue into the
throat and neck.

3

The eyebrows and
outlines of the eyes are
marked in with a black
pencil.

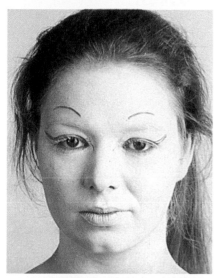

4

These lines are drawn
again in their final
form with black make-
up and a liquid
eyeliner, using an
extremely fine brush.

5

Some white make-up is
applied above the
outline of the upper
eyelid from the inner
corner of the eye to
roughly the middle of
the eye. The same
white make-up is also
applied between the
parallel lines at the
outer corners of the
eyes. Colour in two
small circles of rouge
high up on the
cheekbones fairly close
under the eyes. The
shape of the mouth is
outlined small but
quite high, and this is
then filled in with red
make-up.

6

A geisha wig can be
bought from a novelty
shop and then
enhanced with some
extra dried flowers and
sticks. If the model
does not have a
widow's peak, a
triangle can be
coloured in with black
make-up.

Middle Eastern
(Arab, Jew)

1

Peter without make-up.

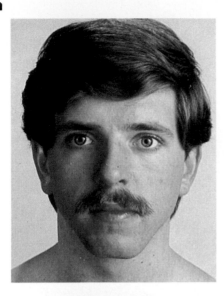

2

A brown foundation is applied to the face right down to the neck.

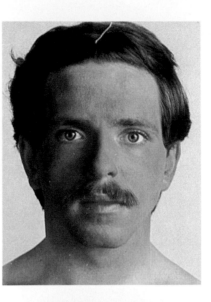

3

Using a brush, dark brown make-up is applied in those places where shadows or folds are required.

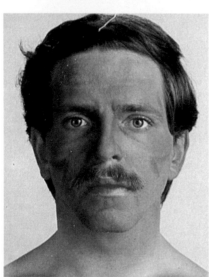

4

When the dark make-up has been blended into the foundation with the finger, a lighter make-up is applied next to the shadows.

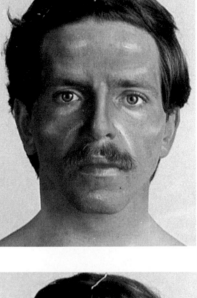

5

This light make-up is also blended into the foundation, though sharp divisions are left to suggest folds. The eyes are firmly outlined with a black pencil. A goatee made of black crêpe hair is stuck down in sections, starting with a tuft under the chin and another tuft on top of this.

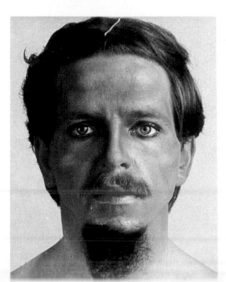

6

This is followed by the last piece, a 'W' shaped tuft cut in advance. Finally, two tufts are stuck down on either side, joining onto the model's own moustache.

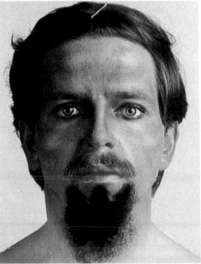

7

The moustache is dyed black with pancake to suggest how it will look when it is cut into shape.

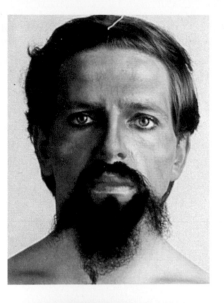

8

The beard is cut into shape. In the example an oval shape has been chosen because this goes well with the model's moustache.

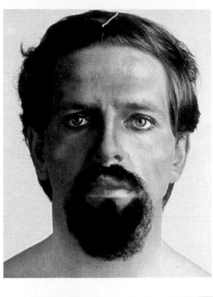

9

The eyebrows, made of black crêpe hair, are stuck down. If necessary, the natural eyebrows could first be coloured black to prevent them showing through. If the model has heavy eyebrows himself, this would suffice.

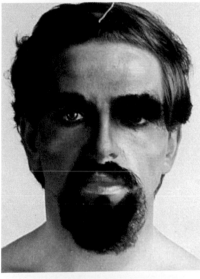

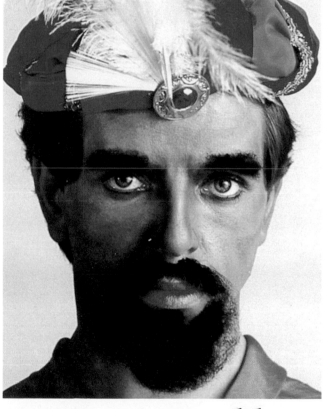

10

The eyebrows are cut into shape and a few extra emphases are added.

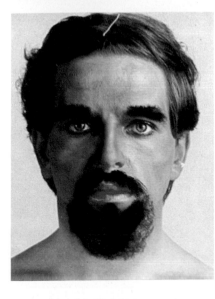

Arabs and Jews have skin of amber olive colour (darker for men, less olive for women). Hair is usually dark and men favor beards and moustaches.

Turban for Arab or Sheik.

11

Finally the model can put on a turban and wear a silk jacket. His own hair has been combed back flat. If the model has lighter hair, this can be darkened with a sponge and then combed.

African/Black

For this make-up it should be remembered that there is just as much variety in Negro faces and features as in Caucasian. If this is not taken into account, you can easily fall into the trap of caricature and the result will be a very crude Black Sambo or Uncle Tom.

To avoid this, always work on the basis of the face that is being made up. Then try to trans-fer typical racial characteristics to the face without turning it into a crude parody. If you work in this way, an individual look can be achieved. In order to give depth to the face it is also better to use highlights than shadows. However, if shadows are necessary, it is best to use a very dark brown almost black colour, though you should always guard against the Black Sambo effect. Try and achieve the most natural possible effect with the make-up.

Skin tones range from light yellowish brown to very dark brown. Their hair is generally frizzy black and often curled or knotted.

1

Karin without make-up.

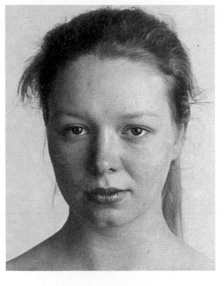

2

A dark brown foundation is evenly applied in two thin layers. The neck is also made up as far as the neckline of the costume to be worn.

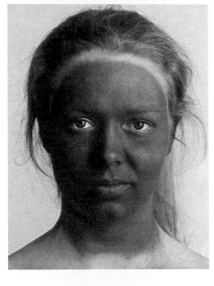

3

Using a golden make-up, highlight the projecting contours. Blend in the gold highlights carefully. Apply some gold along the entire length of the lips.

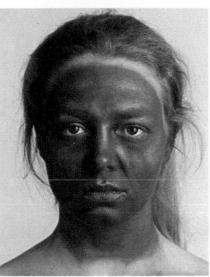

4

The eyes are very carefully outlined with liquid black eyeliner. Some black kohl is applied to the lower eyelids and mascara is used on the eyelashes.

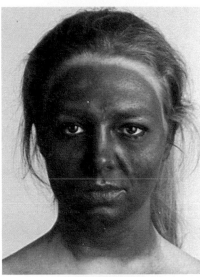

5

You can now choose the eye make-up you want, making sure that the colour is strong enough to show over the dark brown foundation. Use a shiny orangey brown colour on the lips.

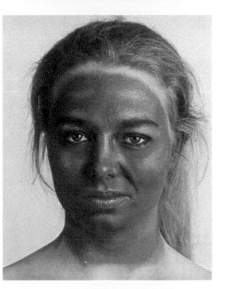

6

Complete the picture with a black curly wig.

American Indian

There are also many different types of faces among Indians. This make-up is for a caricature of the North American Indian; there are two aspects that should be distinguished: First, the typical Indian racial characteristics, in this case sharply defined features (especially the nose, mouth, eyebrows and cheekbones), and secondly the reddish brown colour of the skin. The decoration of the face is also important. Indians use different decorations for different purposes, such as religious rituals, different tribes, and special warpaint. The colours to use are red, blue, green, white and yellow.

INDIAN TALES, Musical, by William-Alan Landes.
(Cheryl Pertile, Marjorie E. Clapper, Sharon Borek, Roz Witt.)

1

Paul without make-up.

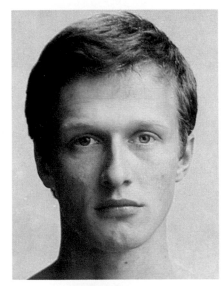

2

A strong reddish brown pancake is applied evenly over the face, neck and shoulders with a damp sponge. The extent to which the make-up should be continued onto the chest, back and arms depends on the costume to be worn.

Skin tones can range from honey colour to reddish and yellowish brown.

3

Using a dark brown make-up, indicate the shadows, lines and folds of the face. The shadows can be quite sharp. Try to keep the face narrow with sharply defined features.

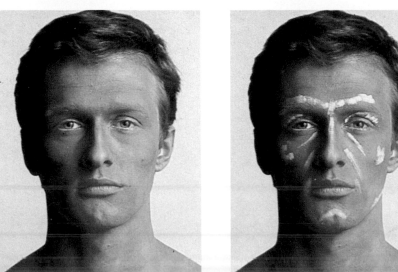

4

A light coloured make-up is applied next to the shadows. Make sure that these highlights are used on the eyebrows and cheekbones.

5

Blend the light make-up into the shadows and foundation with the finger.

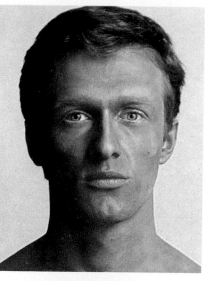

6

Using a black dermatographic pencil, draw in sharply angled eyebrows and boldly outline the eyes.

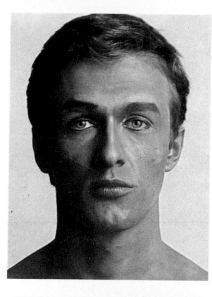

7

The warpaint is applied using red, yellow, white and green make-up. The colours used in the example are based on traditional war colours. Obviously other colours can be used, but do not use too many different ones.

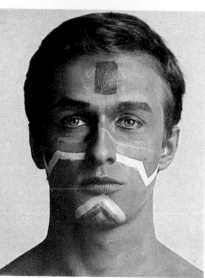

8

A black nylon wig with plaits, which can be bought from a novelty shop, and an embroidered neckband complete the picture.

Little Star Ballet from **INDIAN TALES** by William-Alan Landes. (Randall Mushrush, Sharon Borek, Don Agey, Marjorie E. Clapper, Roz Witt.)

Different types of make-up

Ballet make-up

There are no fixed rules for the make-up used in ballet and this depends entirely on the costume designer and choreographer. There is also a difference between classical and modern ballet, but in general it is true to say that the make-up for ballet should have an enlargening effect, particularly as regards the eyes. The make-up should not be too detailed, and it should be based on the facial structure of the dancer. Thus it is these factors which determine the make-up, rather than the personality. There are many different possibilities, ranging from the large scale make-up used in classical ballet to the smaller scale make-up of modern ballet. The small scale make-up is very similar to normal theatrical make-up, and depending on the interpretation and purpose of the role, it can be elaborated and adapted to be suitable for large ballets. The description given below outlines the steps for classical ballet make-up, but by reducing or omitting some of these instructions it can be modified to suit other types of ballet.

1 Nicole without make-up.

2 A thin pinkish beige foundation is applied to the face, neck and decolleté.

3

The eyebrows are soaped, and when this is dry, make-up is patted on. The whole face is then thoroughly powdered.

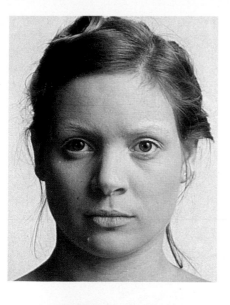

4

The eyebrows are drawn above the natural eyebrows with a liquid eyeliner and an eyeliner brush. These should be wavy and angled towards the hairline. The upper eyelids are also boldly outlined with eyeliner. At the outer corners of the eyes this should be extended upwards parallel to the line of the eyebrow.

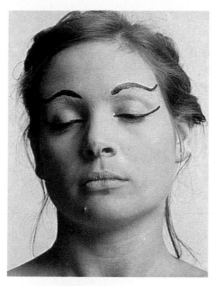

5

The eyeshadow is now applied above the eyeliner. In this example green and gold have been used, but any colour combination is possible, depending on the costume, decor and/or personal taste. Make sure that the lines of the eyeshadow are the same as those used on the eyebrows. This also applies when a number of different colours of eyeshadow are used.

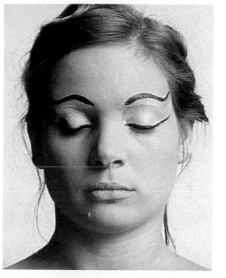

6

The eyeliner used to outline the lower eyelid is not applied immediately below the eyelashes but a little lower. At the inner corners of the eyes particularly it no longer follows the natural shape of the eye. At the outer corners of the eyes the line is extended parallel to the line of the upper eye. White make-up is applied between this line and the eyelashes and between the two lines of eyeliner at the outer corners of the eyes.

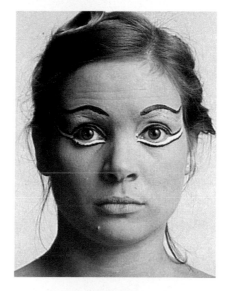

7

False eyelashes are then stuck down on the upper eyelids along the top edge of the eyeliner. These should be stuck slightly higher, just before the outer corners of the eyes. The eyelashes should be no wider than the eyes themselves. A soft rouge is then applied to the cheekbones and thoroughly blended in.

8

Red make-up is used to create full red lips. The hair is combed severely back and is then worn in a bun on the neck.

Charleston (Flapper)

In the 1920s women wore their hair short for the first time in the history of female fashion. At first shoulder length hair was still waved in a tight perm. Later it was worn straight, and finally it was worn very short, almost like a man's hairstyle.

Fashion in clothing was also an obvious protest against the corsets, crinolines and bustles of the past, which were replaced by loose dresses with lowered waistlines. It was also the first time that eyeshadow (in turquoise and blue) and lipstick were used.

1 Karin without make-up.

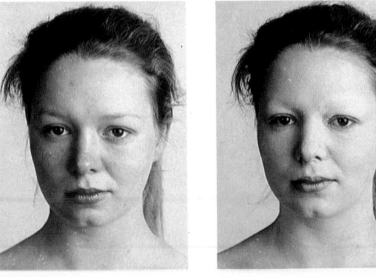

2 A light pinkish beige foundation is applied very thinly and then the eyebrows are soaped. For dark eyebrows it may be necessary to apply an extra layer of make-up.

3

Using a black pencil, mark in the eyebrows slightly above and more rounded than the natural eyebrows. The eyeshadow depends on this shape. First apply a layer over the natural eyebrows. The colour depends on the costume or character.

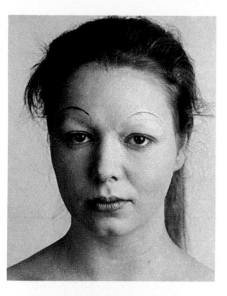

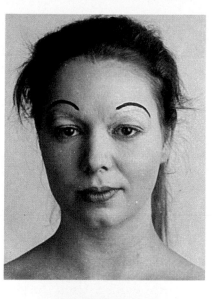

4

Using a black liquid eyeliner, draw in the eyebrows over the pencil lines. The eyeshadow can now be completed in an arch from the inner to the outer corners of the eyes.

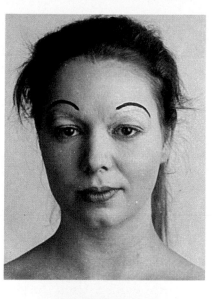

5

Using black eyeliner, the lower and upper eyelids are outlined. A circular patch of rouge is applied high up on the cheekbones. The mouth is filled in as a small heart shape using a carmine red colour.

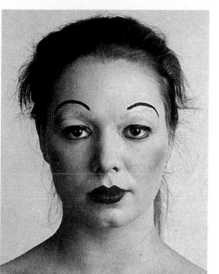

6

A black sequin can be stuck down with eyelash glue just above the mouth. A smooth black nylon wig cut absolutely straight is worn, and the make-up is completed with a headband made of strass and a velvet neckband.

Plays and Musicals where this style of make-up can be used:

CABARET
SUGAR
I AM A CAMERA
ROARING 20's

Drag

The make-up here is used to change a man into a woman, which is the most usual form of drag.

However, it is also possible for a woman to dress as a man.

Up to the end of the seventeenth century it was common throughout Western Europe for women's roles to be played by men, or preferably by boys with unbroken voices. Women were not permitted to act on stage and the theatre was purely a man's domain.

The most famous of these roles were in Shakespeare's plays, and he also made use of a double sex change in which a boy actor acting the part of a woman would then have to pretend to be a boy.

Some of the famous roles of our own time include Danny La Rue and Dustin Hoffman as 'Tootsie'.

For a man to change into a woman the first thing to do is obviously to disguise the male characteristics (such as beard growth) as much as possible.

In a theatrical role it is obviously also very important for the actor to imagine that he is a woman and to adapt his behaviour accordingly. The example described here is based on the most natural possible transformation. Obviously it is also possible to emphasize or enlarge particular features or create a caricature; for example, by exaggerating the eye shadow, eyelashes, rouge or mouth.

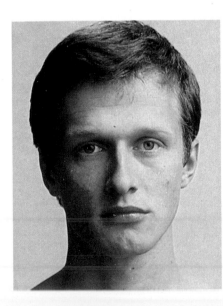

1

Paul before the transformation.

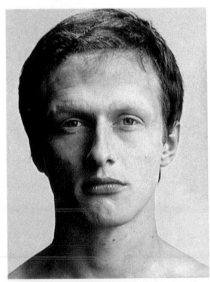

2

The eyebrows are soaped flat against the skin. Then a camouflaging cream is used on the jaws, chin, and above the upper lip to neutralise the beard shadow. A little bit of this cream is also used over the soaped eyebrows.

3

A pale pinky beige foundation is applied over the camouflage on the face and also on the neck.

 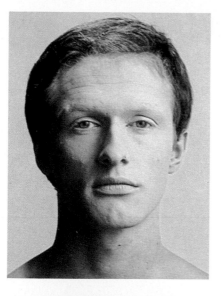

4

A pale eyeshadow is applied to the upper eyelid and over the eyebrow. In this example a golden moss green eyeshadow has been chosen, but the choice of colour depends on the character or type of woman being portrayed. Use a brown pencil to mark in the eyebrows above the natural eyebrows and above the eye shadow.

5

Outline the edge of the eyelashes on the upper eyelids with black liquid eyeliner and apply some kohl above the lower lashes on the edge of the lower eyelid. Then stick down some thin eyelashes on the upper eyelids.

6

A soft red make-up is thinly applied on the cheekbones as rouge. This should be thoroughly blended into the foundation. Use a bright red colour on the lips, making sure they are sharply outlined.

7

The make-up is completed with a red nylon wig and a flower behind the ear.

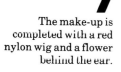 

Plays and Musicals where this style of make-up can be used:

LA CAGE AUX FOLLES
SUGAR
CHARLIE'S AUNT

Fantasy make-up

This category covers a wide variety of make-up including large motifs using exceptional colours, as well as entire masks incorporating a number of small extra motifs. A number of different possibilities are described below, but first a list of general guidelines is given.

– Always take into account the shape of the face. For example, do not use narrow vertical decorations on a long face or horizontal motifs (glitter, sequins, feathers etc.) on a wide or square shaped face.
– Do not use diagonal lines or divisions on the face which run between the eyes. This has the effect of dividing the face in two in an unflattering way.
– Similarly, do not divide the face vertically down the middle unless this is the specific intention of the make-up; for example, to show day on the left and night on the right, or summer and winter at the same time. When small motifs are used, such as flowers or plants, avoid the mouth. Strange distortions otherwise occur in the expression.
– This also applies to the eyes. Do not use vertical lines or divisions over the eyes.
– Try to keep a balance between the left and right halves of the face.
– Work in the width as well as the length.
– Always use a light foundation, so that the colours show up well.

Fanatasy in blue.

Many variations of this particular fantasy face are possible. It is particularly suitable for a masked ball or carnival. It could also be used to portray the theme: queen of the night.

1

Armanda without make-up.

2

A light coloured bluish mauve pancake is evenly applied over the face as a foundation.

3

Using a blue dermatographic pencil, mark in the pattern to be used around the eyes and mouth.

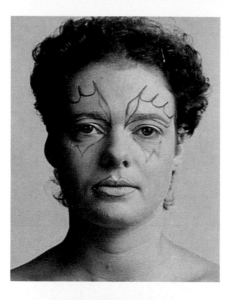

4

The spaces are now filled in and sharply outlined with a brush and bright blue pancake.

5

A few accents are marked in the blue pattern above the eye with dark blue pancake. Dark blue make-up is also used on the upper eyelid in a wide line running down to the nose. The lips are clearly outlined in dark blue.

6

Use a silver greasepaint to put in some counter accents above the eyes, or outline below the eyes. The silver can also be applied in the middle of the pattern on the cheeks in the same shade.

7

Paste stones are stuck down with eyelash glue in the points of the patterns round the eyes. Silver glitter gel is very thinly spread over the entire face with the emphasis on the forehead, edge of the jaw, and lips.

8

A hairpiece of dyed sisal complements this make-up very well. The hard edge has been set off with grey pearls, which have also been used in the crown of the sisal wig.

Silver and black fantasy 1

Nicole without make-up.

2

A pinkish white foundation is applied thinly but evenly.

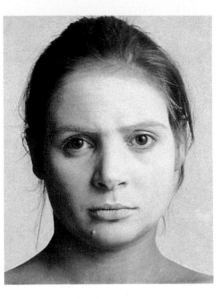

3

When the face has been dusted with a pearly white powder, the patterns are firmly drawn in with silver greasepaint. First mark the patterns in with a very fine brush, preferably using silver make-up. The same applies to the black patterns; they can be marked with a black pencil and then filled in with black pancake. The eyes are outlined with black liquid eyeliner and the lips are coloured with silver make-up.

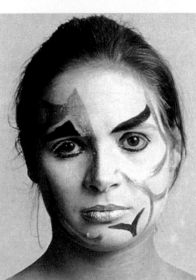

4

A silverfoil wig from a novelty shop and a silver foil collar complete the fantasy effect.

Peking mask

1

This is a free interpretation of the make-up used for one of the masks in the Peking Opera. These masks have been used for centuries. They were described in books and depicted on small wooden heads. Whichever actor plays a particular role wears the mask belonging to that role.

Martin without make-up.

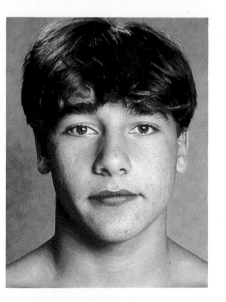

2

Cut a glatzan to size and carefully stick down the edges. Then mark in the pattern with a black dermatographic pencil, keeping it as symmetrical as possible. Using a different brush for every colour, apply the pancake along these pencil lines.

3

Elaborate this pattern as far as possible from the top downwards to prevent smudging. This also makes it easier to check the balance of the lines and colours.

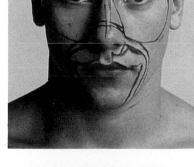

5

Make a beard of dyed sisal twisted round a length of wire. This can be hung round the ears like a pair of spectacles and can be moved, depending on the position of the mouth.

4

This is the complete mask. The ears and neck have not been made up because a beard is worn. If no beard is worn, the ears and neck should also be made up, down to the costume.

Fantasy in green

This is a fantasy make-up which can be used for a wood spirit or futuristic head. It is not a standard make-up but an idea based on a number of different materials such as pearly make-up and various types of glitter. Obviously some of these elements can be left out or others added. It is also possible to use a different colour combination, such as blue or mauve and purple. It is a good idea to base the make-up on the particular colour which can then be used in all sorts of different shades and nuances.

Requirements: mid-green foundation, four different shades of green greasepaint, a dark green pencil, green glitter in dry form and in gel form.

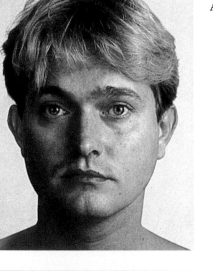

1 Ad without make-up.

2 Apply green pancake to the face as a foundation with a sponge. Apply it evenly, as thicker and thinner patches result in a patchy appearance.

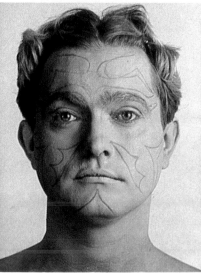

3 Using a dark green dermatographic pencil, draw in the outlines of the pattern on the foundation. Check in the mirror that the pattern is more or less symmetrical. It is impossible for it to be completely symmetrical as the face is not symmetrical.

4

Using a bright green greasepaint, fill in the pattern. On the left some green glitter is applied over it. If dry glitter is used, the brush should be damp so that it is not spilled. The eyebrows, chin and cheek are filled in with a golden green glitter.

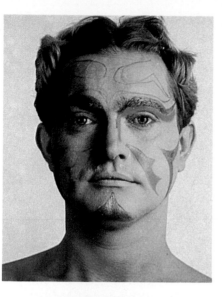

5

Using a different shade of green, fill in the pattern on the forehead and again put some glitter onto this immediately. Other patterns are now outlined with a spray of green glitter gel.

6

The mouth is made up in a pattern that fits in with the other patterns on the face. A sprinkling of glitter adds depth and glitter is also used on the eyebrows.

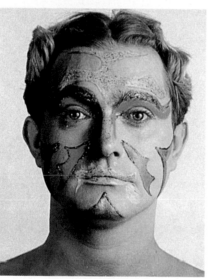

7

The eyes are outlined in dark green make-up. Check that the complete pattern is well balanced and if necessary, correct an unevenness by emphasising certain lines.

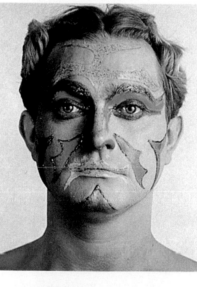

8

The make-up can be completed with a nylon wig from a novelty shop and some green pieces of material.

9

A completely different result can be obtained with the same make-up, but this time with a sisal headdress and collar.

Clowns and pierrots

Clowns and pierrots appear in a great variety of roles, sometimes as acrobats or as musicians.

However, in all their acts they hold up a mirror to the public to reflect their character and stimulate laughter.

Circus clowns date back further than pierrots. They first appeared in England during the second half of the eighteenth century, when circuses began to replace fairs, originally as horse parades. Many artists who appeared at fairs and festivals in the open air joined this sort of circus. Clowns developed particularly in England and also in Russia.

The nineteenth century Pierrot, also known as the clown de luxe or the white clown, was a creation of the French mime artist, Deburau, and was inspired by the sixteenth century figure of Predolino from the Italian Commedia dell'arte. Pierrots and clowns played opposite each other and the contrast between the clever pierrot and the stupid or naive clown is very important. Because of the many different characters there is no one specific make-up for clowns and pierrots and the make-up is left largely to the clown's own imagination. However, it is always advisable not to overdo the make-up and get bogged down in detail. The neat figure of the elegant Pierrot has thin stylised eyebrows, sometimes two different eyebrows. A distinction can be made between a happy and a sad Pierrot by drawing the lines of the eyebrows, round the eyes, and the corners of the mouth, upwards or downwards.

Circus clown

1
Luppo without make-up.

See: **STRUTTER'S COMPLETE GUIDE TO CLOWN MAKEUP,** Players Press 1991.

2
Draw in the pattern of the eyes and mouth with a black dermatographic pencil.

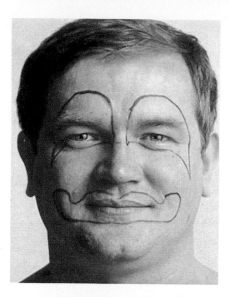

3
Using a brush and white pancake, go round the pencil lines to make sure that they are sharply drawn.

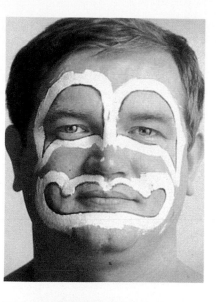

4
The rest of the face is now painted an even white colour. This can be done with a wide brush or with a sponge. In both cases watch out for lines or unevennesses.

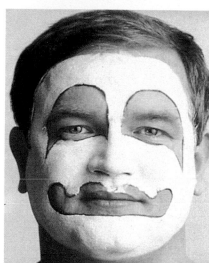

5
The spaces round the eyes are filled in with orange greasepaint and the mouth with bright red greasepaint. Take care not to go over the pencil lines or the white greasepaint.

6
The black pencil lines are now drawn over with a fine brush and black liquid eyeliner. Two vertical lines are drawn over the upper eyelids from the edge of the eyelashes to above the eyebrows; the eyes are sharply outlined and small black lines mark the creases that appear when laughing, at either side of the mouth.

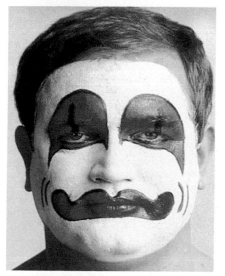

7
In this example a curly yellow wig is used, but any other party or clown wig can be used with the make-up. The same applies to the hat and costume, and the photograph shows just one example.

Pierrot

1

Rafael without make-up.

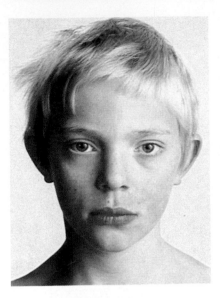

2

The whole face is coloured white with two layers of pancake. The first layer is brushed on and when it is dry, the second layer is patted on.

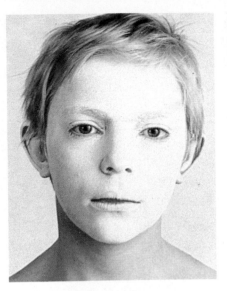

3

The patterns are carefully drawn in with a black pencil. Check in the mirror that they are in the right position on the face.

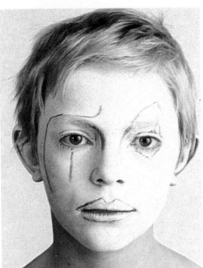

4

The pencil lines are now drawn over with a black pancake or liquid eyeliner and a very fine brush. The eyes and mouth are also outlined and the mouth is filled in with carmine red make-up. Make sure that the black lines are as sharp and uncluttered as possible.

5

Silver sequins are stuck down at the points of some of the black lines. These are available from drapers' shops. A black sequin is stuck down above the corner of the mouth. The make-up is completed with a Pierrot hat.

See: **STRUTTER'S COMPLETE GUIDE TO CLOWN MAKEUP,** Players Press 1991.